T0277711

ANY MOONWALKER CAN TELL YOU:

new and selected poems

JOEL PECKHAM

STEPHEN F. AUSTIN STATE UNIVERSITY PRESS

Production Manager: Kimberly Verhines
Cover Art: Lily Jurskis

ISBN: 978-1-62288-256-4

For more information:
Stephen F. Austin State University Press
P.O. Box 13007 SFA Station
Nacogdoches, Texas 75962
sfapress@sfasu.edu

Distributed by the Texas A&M University Press Book Consortium
www.tamupress.com

First Edition

CONTENTS

For Rachael and Darius

NIGHTWALKING

Moontide on the Inland Sea

Quiet, quiet, they drift and rock, tug at their moorings,
then freed by darkness, slide out, silent running.
The possum, the raccoon, the cat, tremulous, hesitant
at first, settle into swells and ride a current to distant
streets, launches driven in a strong breeze
full with salt-sweat, the oceanic roar of leaves,
of paper, of plastic grocery bags, a child's t-shirt caught
in the branches and flapping, flickering, slack then taut.
Ages ago, millennia, they say that this was all a vast
inland sea where ancient creatures hungered in shallows
—a comfort to one who, all his life, watched the masts
rise and loom on the horizon, far from shore, from home.
There is sustenance out here, quivering and wet.
I spread my fingers to the waters; I am casting my nets.

In The Beginning

It is not the word, but the word's
anticipation, caught in the lungs, in the windpipe, passing
through all stays, all stops and come on roughly as sheer
sound: an infant screams in the apartment across the hall,
two young men groan in the attic above; grackles crowd
the dying oak with fitful noise. We hear the fits and starts,
the seductive callings of the town as they lead us, slipping in
like shadows over the couch that rots on a neighbor's lawn,
over a sleeping child out past curfew, up the concrete steps
of the Congregational church where a transient rattles
the door-chain, and further, beyond all walls, into the open
places of the church itself, the mind's-eye of the child
and her guiltless dreams of the minister's long white throat.
These are the makings of borders and of border crossings,
the fittings and unfastenings of treacherous ground where pressure
builds in the pipes, a door slams brightly as the street vanishes
in shades of blue, and we are left waiting, wanting like lovers
exploring each other with their hands, their mouths, knowing
something is about to happen, something magical.

Nightwalking

I'm walking out into the town
I've never visited, down a darkened street
I've traveled all my life. Where lamp lights
burn on one by one, possum skitter out
on cool tar in a night become a blanket of heat
and sound— cicadas, the suffering of crickets,
houses swelled with sleep— a trembling
in and out, child-breath, leaf-shudder.

It is getting late.

And more dangerous. It can't be helped.
Every child knows there are no safe places
any longer. Even here, under the blanket,
in a town I form with every step. With every
breath. I watch the possum, cornered
by my shadow, back up against a wall,
scream like an infant, then break
for shelter.

"O" Street, Lincoln NE

You have heard the rumor that this street ends somewhere
past the railroad tracks, petering out with the last
of the asphalt before a river, or a cornfield, or in a distant city
at the edge of Iowa. Don't believe it. How can nothing pass
into nothing without continuation? This is a street where no-one
lives but everyone works, where every breath is windblown,
and like paper driven past the stoplights over the rise
in the hill to the blackened windows of a "gentlemen's club"
where a neon woman, mouth open, whispers the lie— we want you
here, anything can be bought. Streets like this go on, endless
in the urban sprawl of every dying city in America. So I will speak
of it as a kind of prayer for the empty house on the corner of 27th,
with the sloping porch and *For Sale* sign hanging loose from the door,
everyone knowing it will not be sold or occupied, knowing
that my words, with nothing left to stop them, will reach beyond
the Wyuka Place of Rest—est. 1869, beyond the Forbidden City
oriental restaurant, the Texaco, Robbins Mortuary, past the Gateway
Mall, beyond this town, down the river, through cornrows, to reach
another road—highway 80 or 35 and pick up speed, all the way through
Pennsylvania, to New York to the Atlantic and then straight
to the ears of God— a prayer of continuation, of existence,
traveling the corridors of the throat saying, *O* and again *O* and *O, O, O.*

The House on the Corner

of 21st and B needs more
than a fresh coat of paint, more than the green vine
that creeps through seams in the concrete, slow, insistent,
as music rising from the basement (a blues played bad
but hard by a man grown old with a song of all that is
not yet lost, all that is not quite wrong, but still
unbearable, and rising in his bones, his fingertips)
toward the attic room where a young boy,
sweating in a twist of sleep and sheet and streetlight,
has his first wet dream (of no-one he has ever known
or seen—not the other boys or girls down the street,
not their mothers, throats taut
and quavering with evening and children too far off
to hear, not his mother miles and miles away
in another town, in another home)—a dream that is
wholly body touching body, silent, palpitant, as the same
few notes played over and over with slightest variation
beneath him in a house that for a moment needs
the strain that lives between the beats, between the father
and the son and the mother, and the dark breathing town,
— the pulse that reaches, touching barely, gently, and is
moving, always moving away.

Mud Season

The thing about remembering is that you don't forget—— Tim O'Brien

Vermont. Ripton. It comes when the ground gives way
from six tight months of frost— red clay, soil, dung, softened
with the moan of aspens and the oak relaxing into April
as a hard man's fist unclenches from a ten-pound maul.
At evening. With darkness. And you can't keep it out.
Creeping into boot leather, canvas, jeans, your skin. Following
you home, across the fields, into your house, floorboards,
bed sheets, years of dreams. Where people have lost things—
whole fields of boots pulled down and smothered, chainsaws,
wheelbarrows, left out, sunk, taking root. Once
behind the old barn, down the sloping pasture where
the east field meets the spring I watched a team of men
struggling to pull a horse from the earth. His forelegs lost
to the kneecaps, his chest down and forward as if
he were bending to drink, or was caught in descent, leaping
a fence—a moment's grace where time doesn't seem
to move or matter—but there was no grace in this. He fought
or tried to fight, pulling against his own weight which only
made each leg sink deeper. I remember the whites of his teeth
and eyes bared clear, whiter with fear and muck. I remember
the sound of screaming, throaty, desperate—the ropes tightening
around his waist, his legs, and the men pulling, digging, cursing
the mud, the horse, the rain, themselves and sinking still. And I
remember thinking they were all part of the same beast, brown
and heaving from the earth as if a great oak were trying to uproot
itself from the banks and walk. It was dark and raining. I was
cold and colder for being young and younger for being hopeful.

Don't ask me how this story ends. You know. And even now
the telling feels like a sinking in. Miles away, years gone and still
when I hear the loud crack of branches in a March storm, I feel it
in my chest, a breaking in the breath hitting full force, a gunshot
hovering somewhere in the tree-limbs. And I know that I
won't sleep or worse, will—having given in to the night,
to exhaustion like some great heaving animal, its legs broken,
closing his eyes at last, sinking into the earth.

Loonsong

Out into the cold
a loon calls to its mate.

Steam rises on the water.
I think of my father misting the window

of the old green Chevrolet with scraps
of Nat King Cole and Velvet Fog

on the long drive to the nursing home.
We earn the ache that waits for us

somewhere past the final note.
The moon blows back a brassy chord

on the pond's black skin

When I Dream of Eternity

It's like this: late September
and all along the stone shore—Camden, Rockport,
Booth Bay, Bar Harbor—the boats are drifting home
with the almost human scent of rotting fish and sweat.
The tourists are gone—the young girls, arms naked
and burning in the sun—the boys who chased them
in old cars, hot and sulfurous. The vendors have closed
up shop. And the town is left to the abandoned
shipyard, its rails empty and running into darkness,
to piled lobster traps that dry and rot, to the second
mortgage, the grocery bill, to the bone-white spire
of the Lutheran church reflected in bay water,
engine-sleek and shining with the last flame
of evening. There is the hungry cry of gullsong,
a hollow report of wood on wood and the quiet
chatter of the last ones on the docks, tying off
their boats, shoulders swaying drunk with work
— unbreakable, timeless, they will make this season
last as long as they can. Forever if they have to.

Beginning to See

— For Susan— teacher, painter, poet, wife, expectant mother . . .

Here, in the apartment where the air smells of iron—lofted
from the furnace through old ducts, through dusty, rusted vents
— carried quietly into small rooms where the walls cringe
and groan against a February wind. Here on his knees in a room
alive with echoes—her breathing, the soft rise and fall of water,
sounding strangely like laughter, like the laughter of children
— he bends above her— because she is five months along
and cannot bend to slide the blade across her calves, her ankles
—trying to be careful, he thinks

of his father, strong hands guiding a blade
across the delicate skin of his throat, his chin— like this: long strokes,
quick, clean—thinks of his mother by the lake in Maine, skirts lifted
barely, soap traveling away from her ankles, clouding
the sky's bright reflection.
                                    She laughs at him, her belly
blooming against the water— too gentle, the bathwater cooling. And she,
dizzy from the sour scent of air, remembers— far away, away in a country
where the air smells of roof-tar, boiling in the summer heat, roof-tar
and the strong scent of sugar boiling in vats in the kitchen
—and the women laughing and yelling out as they apply the wet cloths
to their legs— pull and scream, pull and scream, and telling
their stories.

                    And as she tells him, he begins to see, drifting in
by degrees like his great-grandfather in the study— reading perhaps,
or staring at a photograph, a ray of sun on the back of his neck
— an old man falling asleep slipping deliciously in. And there he is

with the morning prayers rising in the city and the sound of laughter
all around him, the women bending over, legs bared and blooming,
speaking in a language that sounds strangely like the rise and fall
of water and his wife, a young girl, now, running between—aunt

to mother to grandmother, and back and laughing, laughing

She shouts—careless, blood blooms to her thigh
and he is saying, I am sorry, thinking of the stone's round shadow
reaching out into the lake, sunfish rippling the water's skin,
thinking of the minarets and domes that reach high above the city
the sound of prayer, holy and rising.
                                        In the apartment where the air
smells like iron—here in the dead center of America, he reaches
thinking *Beautiful, Beautiful where else will you lead me?*

THE HEAT OF WHAT COMES

Traffic

You are now entering Kansas
Or another state just like it—bumper sticker

They're out there. Cursing, pleading with the radio,
watches flashing with sun. Stagnant pools form
between the shoulders beneath a business suit—a hundred,
a thousand business suits, pantsuits, working casuals.
At the temples, a vein begins to swell. In Pennsylvania,
a bridge shudders under the weight of waiting cargo:
boxes of food, frozen in dry ice, arteries blooming
with soot and smoke and the accumulated heat
of prayer: *Please God, I have* a meeting, a wedding

a ballgame, a doctor's appointment, and the needle
pushes into red toward empty. Or hot. Necks strain
to find a gap the eyes can pass through. Someone
stares at a map, mumbling names of roads, 128, 80,
75, Route 2, 31, 15. They are all impassable,
impossible as the long passage of cornrows shook
with summer wind. In the breakdown lane, bent
under the hood, someone is waving his hands at steam

as if warding off imaginary wasps, ghosts, the broken
lines that stretch through tunnels and off-ramps, high
over rivers and other roads and deep into the sides
of mountains. In darkness a small boy wonders
what kinds of tools it took, what kinds of people
to head into a wall of earth and come out again
—earth-fired, beaming—wonders if he can or will. In Ohio
a woman tastes iron in the air, rolls up the window.
For there are signs, there always are, some green, some

white. Shaking with shaken roads and words submerged
in haze that on a clear night with the road open would
emerge like prophecy: 20 MILES TO THE GREAT

DIVIDE. 30 MILES TO NIAGARA FALLS. 240 MILES TO
DISNEY WORLD. IDAHO WELCOMES YOU. AMERICA
BEGINS HERE: in PARIS MAINE, pop.134, GENEVA
TEXAS, or MONTICELLO ARKANSAS. They are here,
they are coming, stalled and running From Lichfield
to Holland. Bucksnort to Bulls-Gap to Leavenworth where

the Suburban on 35 has been entering Kansas
for hours. And the Subaru traveling north may never leave
Illinois. Even the cab driver on the Garden State has gone
silent gone hoarse—sick of traffic reports and alternate routes
he doubts anyone has been to. They aren't telling. Aren't coming
back. And even if you got out of the car, hopped the median, scaled
the soundproof barrier to the well-manicured lawns of Saddle River
or Newton, what then? Who would be there for you? Better to wait
with the sound off, think of a girl you knew in high school, sitting
by some other sign on some other road, her daughter pleading to go
to the bathroom. Or think of other roads that must lead somewhere

after all, with so many of them on the way
to someplace or another
just like it.

In the Next Seat:

At the Greyhound Station, Nashville TN

A man sits in stink. The little girl
asleep against his chest has wet
them both from Atlanta through
Chattanooga, and he's
as scared to wake her
as you might be to wake
the dead. Awake could be
anything: could be vomit, or
weeping or the non-stop
chatter of the wired. And how
we would all wish for sleep now;
how a stink in dreams can seem
to break things down, mingle
salt, piss, deodorant, gasoline,

distance. Too much
distance. A little girl sleeping
on a man's lap in middle
Tennessee can be
a thousand things, all of them
having everything and nothing
to do with the woman
in the second row who keeps
wanting to know why we need
"to stop at every piece of shit,
podunk nothing town from here
to Alaska" or the man who says,
dead serious, "this bus don't go
there, only to Gary, you'll
have to catch another," or
how I need to go

to the bathroom and don't know
if I can climb the seat in front

of me without hitting some sleeping
arm or leg with a knee, a stray
foot. So I think of how John Glenn,
pissing in his spacesuit, swore
he saw something bright and alive

through the window of his capsule,
fireflies, living sparks, wheeling,
dancing in the void. How it was
only dust, backlit and shining

with a million stars. So sealed off
or in, we wish for any kind of contact
and fear it. Coming over the hills
of Chattanooga, looking for shadows
in the wood, or into moonroofs
into windshields, into the eyes of neon
signs where Sam is always sad and Charlie,
nervous, and fireworks can be had
for a couple of dollars a dozen,
with boiled peanuts, and diesel fuel.

But the sparks are only headlights
gliding on a mirrored surface,
and our own eyes staring back,
heavy and lurching as any bus
that never seems to want
to get going again. In no
particular hurry to let the air
rush in and leave this place
because it carries everything
along: the man beside me,
the little girl, the stink
of any life that breathes
just near you but is not
yours, could never be, like any
answer, or any distant dream
of sleep.

Asleep at the Wheel

— We must love each other or die, Auden

I'm driving home from Atlanta, down 441—an unlit
stretch of highway winding through lakes and fields,
and I am fighting sleep—on the radio
someone explains the reasons for war.

I think of the photographs on CNN—gaunt Afghanis,
Palestinians. Kids—staring out the bombed out shells
of their bodies. Wide awake, too awake, with hunger
and fear. As a boy I remember most the dark unblinking
glitter of the eyes of fish—a rich obsidian depth that reached
back and down like canyons off Rockland—gleaming
with moving water and the reflections of leaves,
of quahog shells, of bright stones and the caught
gleam of sunlight in a torn can—or the gaze of anyone
leaning over the hull so far he almost tumbles into
gravity, longing, the deadly bliss

of children. Like too small fish shaken from trawl-nets
at pre-dawn, my sons, flicker in oncoming beams
and disappear—the darkness slides across them,
takes them, throws them back into light again. And again,

I'm holding the baby against me. His first illness and
I'm terrified. His skin kindles mine—a gull caught
in old netting. His flail and scream against a sinking
down, a falling out of the world. In the distance,

the town sleeps and dreams of small things, grasses bend
and rise again in river-water the way the head of a young boy
strapped upright in a car will loll and jerk back, loll
—a rhythmic, sickly dance that's hard to look at, too fragile
and human—like eyelids fluttering on a field of white
and the deep rich blackness of irises wide in sleep. I bite
my lip. There are no shoulders, no medians. We are

so near, and hurtling by each other
at great speed.
        And what was the name again
of the desert saint who, starving, came upon a vision
of a lion feasting on his own leg. Or a lamb, or
the saint himself. I can't remember, but it seems

important now.

Living in Layers:
in memory of Cyrus, Mesozoic Gallery, Morrill Hall, U of Nebraska

A shout and mammoths shudder.
Bones which once frightened you
to desperate weeping seem
to quiver as you run, back and across
and forward again, like some sunblown
shell on white sandstone. That light
and blinding. Son, we are walking
again through ages, me reverent, solemn,
you skipping, dancing, in and out
of the ropes which cordon off,
the dead from the dead from the living.

—*Jurassic, Paleolithic, Mesozoic*— and you

stop—in the gallery of the great inland
waterway where walls shudder
with an ancient sea—the artist
stopping jaws in hunger on the spines
of sharks, eyes (so many eyes) glassed in
with something like longing. But this
does not matter to a boy lost in some

strange cold thrill on a Midwest Saturday
morning in July; what matters is the stone
beneath your feet, beneath the plexiglass
partition where bones of a Great Bulldog
Tarpin swim eternally northward,
block-jawed and dangerous. You jump

back and scream in fear,
                    no,
                         delight, then
stomp and stomp and stomp on the glass
as if to shake the fish, the walls, the sea itself

to life with all its ages and no one to stop you.

The Heat of What Comes

I remember one winter

the wind coming full bore off Misquamicut,
so the plate-glass hummed with it and I thought
I felt the house shudder free of its mooring and drift
for days of heavy snow and rain. So I knew when
I went walking or lay in bed awake, that it was all

different. And always like this. The town ripped
from its foundation, sliding and slipping over a deep

and unknown sea. That was a long way back, and I
only remembered it just now. But now it changes

everything. It found me.

As in a symphony: once you've heard it, the change:
the choral part: that oboe, or tonal color lurks from
the start like a small animal on the edge of your
porch-light—the way Mozart's burial in a mass grave

lurks in his Requiem. In the Don. In Figaro. In the first
moment his father handed him a violin. Waiting
for him, for us, to find it. And I know how fire kindled
in the peat of old forests can burn beneath the ground
for weeks without anyone knowing. Only the scent
of burning and the fox feeling it beneath her feet: warm

and humming—and dangerous.

Sometimes

1.
While the rain ticks the hour on the tin roof and the heron
strides slowly on wet leaves by the water line, I can feel
the slip and run down the drainpipe,
the sloughing and sucking of all things—the longing
of the homebound at the end of the street, the longing of the divorcée
finally abandoned after years of bitterness, and the little boy
who doesn't even understand what he has lost, playing
in the backyard a week after his mother died,
pointing to a contrail in a clear blue sky—the way we suffer,
pulled and pushed by the looking backward while moving
forward against our wills, that gangly walk
that long legged stride.

2.
Like most of us there is so much I would
rephrase, revise, unreel, undo, burn through like the film
on the old projector my father never quite learned
to operate, swearing, his hands suddenly desperate,
to hit the right switch to patch and splice as these
illusions of life curl and yellow toward the edges.

And the house seems almost to empty itself, the boxes
fill on their own accord, the moving truck idles
in the driveway and what goes on goes on
in spite of us.

3.
sometimes sometimes sometimes I swear
when the wind is right and the lake turned velvet and alive
like the chilled skin of a lover after love and the breath once
quick and gasping quiets and settles like a leaf on winter snow

the woods will bend and strain at once and

I can almost hear the bitter laughter of the boughs.

The Fog Warning
— for Gordon Peckham, Alzheimer's Victim, 1982

Even the halibut—white, headless, piled, and stacked seem alive with this:

the dory stilled and rising, crested on a stopped wave

the rower's muscles caught in flex

oars glisten but do not touch a water that could be iron but is not, is alive

no sea spume lifts in the air, nor falls

—far off over his shoulder the blurred image of a ship.

Farther, the dark and sudden clouds

perhaps he thinks of a child playing in the yard

or of a lover he crept from in the crevasse of a dark years off

or your grandfather staring,

standing in a frozen parking lot somewhere

in Massachusetts with his test results—knowing for the first time that his mind

will leave him cell by dying cell—the memories

of children, then the names, then nothing

but the roaring tidal sound of his own blood and the shattered, shattering

scream of gulls.

        The moment.

The forced calm and set jaw of one who knows that we

                               are too far out

far gone and the warning that was

                          too late could not have been

otherwise and the fog

                this fog is coming.
                        Recognition. Here

                                          it is.

Here.

The Fog People

What is remarkable is not how many have been lost,
drifting and starved, but the number who survive.

The child who walked off into the mist

becoming the ache in the center of his father's hands as he pushed
the long-handled broom down darkening corridors of light,

the last few miles on the highways home to some northern city,

the last thoughts of a woman crumpled in her car, drunk with pain
and crying herself to sleep

sands and seas

the luminescent graying of the sky

steps back onto the beach, into our lives— or comes out somehow
on the other side of it all,

with the knowledge of the willow shaken to the roots
by light rain

a rain of light

footsteps on the dock

— a cane tapped down the street, searching

for echoes—

Even now they are stirring, they are waking

Listen, how the lovers find each other with their hands, their mouths

pull back

and touch.

Walking Through Fog:

      Once when the house was dark and silent, asleep, I woke
to Susan in the bathroom door, naked and giving back streetlight,
dream-sigh, the midnight voice of grass

      and it shook me bodily and straight down as if the walls
had been blown-through, sea-sifted and the air palpable

      with trillium reaching across the lawn, dew-cold, and salted
with the salt of the body, alive and shivering with the last breath held
in the lungs of the last wild elk in North America,

      with the stretch and creak of the barked sapling, livid

      with our worst fears of heaven

      where one might walk forever in silence over open ground: arms
outstretched exactly like this:

      like some blind bird of prey:

      some searchlight searching for decades over flat, black water:

      surge, and urge, and seethe

Dearest,

      I have seen the light slowly shatter through the hallways
and the highways with all the roads and road signs, and the calls of birds,
and walked on anyway anywhere, with the empty stare of the walker in the fog,
driven only by fear, hunger, and the body-glow of memory

      there is no more distance than this:

      no more touching than this:

the eagle feeling for the first time in his feathers in his wings,

a slight disturbance in the depths

in the air

trillium and trellis vine,

and all the secret reachings of the sea.

What to Say

In the long moment after love with her arm under your arm,
her fingers at your chest, her hips moving a little behind you, your
bodies still warm and flushed, when she says, *Lover?* and you
murmur *yes* and she says *how did you learn to touch*
a woman. First lie there a moment, take your time, thank
whatever God you worship but take care of how you answer.
Don't puff out your chest and lower your voice like Elvis.
Don't say *Trial and error baby.* Don't tell her about that
older woman at the bar when you were twenty who took your
hand beneath her blue velvet skirt. Don't talk of some
book you read as a boy. And never *never* bring up porn. If you're
a man who likes porn which means you probably haven't
been asked this question anyway. No— tell her where all touchings
start. On the edge of a beach as a child, the burning
sand in your toes, salt on your tongue, shorts clinging and that
first feeling, first stirring of blood. Tell her how you always
loved the feel of the world. Tell how, in the store with your
mother, you'd push your hands in the racks of clothes and feel
crinoline, taffeta, cotton, corduroy, satin, silk. How
your tongue would creep to your teeth and slip out and your
mother and your sisters would make fun of you. Let her
laugh because she's seen you do it with her. Tell her
how you'd linger in sleep and roll in that softness for hours.
Tell of the summer when you were thirteen and your parents
got you the paper route, so you could lose that paunch at your
middle— only you didn't because, slick with your own heat
you'd roll into the dairy, feel the cold blast all over you
and order a milkshake so you could feel God's own glory
slip down your throat. How you grew fat and sassy.
Tell her you've always been a hedonist always been touching
the world. Tell her how working one summer as a landscaper you'd go
into woods without your shirt because you liked the tiny scratches,
the feel of the leaves on your back. How you'd plant tulips
and shrubs without gloves so you'd spend days with dirt
beneath your fingernails. Tell her of that time at the bar when

you were 17 and way too young and way too drunk to go home
and you first really *felt* the blues through your feet and the vibration
of the table and the soft touch of that voice all over you, coming
from the stage, from a woman who did not move so much as roll
her body to and away from you, who sang bodily, entering
the microphone, entering you layer by layer. Tell her how
there are days since you met her when you swear you can touch
the wall of any building and feel the lovers in the corner apartment
on the second floor on the west side making love. Tell her
everything you can because you can, and she'll listen. Or better,
don't, because it's not an answer she was looking for;
linger in the silence more. Say *lover,* Say *love,*
and touch and touch and touch.

GOD'S BICYCLE

Body Memory

Once, a boy, out walking the access road along
Route 1, I watched a woman jump (or was she
pushed) from the bed of a truck, her body spun into
fields of tall grass and gravel. And when she rose,
holding her head in her hands, bleeding, standing,
she came up slow, in pain. Unfolding. Every inch
alight in pain. Mouth wide, silent. And the truck
pulling away, the door still open, swinging wild
as it made the corner onto the highway.

Still, I am shocked, not by how fragile
we are, but how easily transformed. Did she
will herself to stand, some signal shouting, *Up
Damnit. Up!* or did she simply find herself
upright again, still stunned to have fallen, to be
this person in this moment, a strange boy
staring at her. I watched for a moment,
thought, *my God* and took off running. Dust

on my tongue—terrified and young and trying
to outdistance the image of one who rose
from the ground, from the surely dead, who swayed
and shook, then, sunstruck, dropped to earth again.

Psalm 96

Sing to the lord a new song—of men and women riding
the last bus home through quarries and yellowing
tobacco fields of highway 421. Sing the long sigh
and slow grind of axles and tired eyes that watch
through glass the memory of Guthrie and Bluff Hills
and the Greenback Labor Party that never had a chance to
sing of strong arms and backs that broke in heat and boys
and girls who'd grow barefoot through stones and stagnant
water and bellies swole with hunger. Sing malaria, pellagra
and the scars that faded and the scars that didn't. Sing
a new song from the old, the way things work their way
like hookworm up and in through cracks in the skin. Sing
their descendants up from the dust to work in Michigan
auto plants and down to dust again in mines of West Virginia.
Sing cornbread and potatoes. Sing food stamps and long lines
and the water shut-off notice on the door. Sing thirst and stink
and the boys signed up to fight through mustard gas and jungle,
the beaches of Europe and the Philippines, the deserts
of the Middle East. Sing of IEDs and what *freedom really means*
to empty bellies and an anger at everything. Sing of sand—
how it gets everywhere—hair, the pits of your arms, groin,
grinding away the skin like hunger gets everywhere. How
sometimes the only thing to put in an empty hand is another
hand. Sing anger and lust and football on cold Friday nights—
the crush of bodies on bodies. Sing full contact and sex
in muscle cars on back country roads and in the basements
and parking lots. Sing of children and more children. 99 cent
burgers and cold fries and grease that fills them. Sing the grease
that makes the stomach clamp. And single mothers who learned
from their mothers whose men were gone before they were gone
even when they were there. Sing cosmetology school, beauty
school and the community college down the road. Because
you're 50 years old and still trying, still singing—man gone,
kids trying to be gone, and you stealing hours on the nursing home
computer where you work wiping asses and cleaning bedpans,

so you can take a night class on *gender issues,* so you can learn
words like patriarchy, hegemony, abject, subaltern. Sing
the privilege you're supposed to have. Sing the spirit. Sing
to the Lord because the Lord is hope that maybe a new song
can rise green and leafy from a bitter soil. Sing, because it's all
you have—this life bound up in other lives before you
that matter because you say they do, you say you do
because you sing.

Movers and Shakers

Lord, let me shake / With purpose
                    —James Dickey, "The Strength of Fields"

Listen, you can hear them—dragging the past
on blankets over smooth wood floors, loading bureaus
on dollies. Clicking, creaking, grunting with effort,
a man descends the stair, eyes forward, chin high, hair
matted with sweat and sighs, a hundred-year-old
hutch strapped to his back. A subtle quiver
in the calves, a tremble in the neck. In the truck
a driver checks and rechecks the list, figures
weight and cost. They always underestimate
and not by a little. Yes, this will cost
a hell of a lot. But who can really figure the way
a life accumulates until it is boxed, stacked,
packed, to fill the yard, the truck

—that's twice as much
as you quoted! Yessir but your weight was off
at least a thousand pounds. We figure
by weight—your piano alone . . . .

                    He has learned to take
their anger the way a fisherman takes weather, a fact
of life, impersonal to him. Anger never is about
the cause. And after all, they have to pay or leave
the marriage bed, the crib, stereo, boxes
of clothes and toys—to sit, overnight or longer
in the drive. Their lives left open to wind,
and rain, the inspection of neighbors—
a judgment worse than God's. Moving is hard
enough. To move is to risk and for what,
to where? So many things piled and poorly
placed. Always on the verge of tipping, shattering
in the dark, the whole living world trembling around.

U-HAUL:

On Highway 65 North of Louisville Kentucky,
the back end of the U-HAUL tries to shake
its caging free from the ache of hands,
a steering column shook with heavy rain.
The lock is loose and steel slams steel
as a bed frame winks and jostles under years
of toys they couldn't bear to leave
behind or give away or toss clanging in the iron
dumpster that bloomed beyond belief, beyond
proportion with their little house, little lives
and plans, and still there is so much—these years
of trunks and clothes that don't fit anyone, packed,
stacked and roped to walls, taking on the hope
of diets and medications and promise green
as grass in another place, another town where
the divan, a bicycle with a broken chain, box springs
the pullout sofa could come to rest again
and live

        (how is it the new start always begins
in the past, going back so far that we keep even
what could break us when what could break us
is so little)

        Somewhere north of Louisville and south
of here—that strange sense it is all too much after all,
that we left something important back there and it is gone
and not gone, shuddering high above and behind and far out
in front of us.

Improvisation for Guitar, Lake Sinclair, GA
— for Cyrus

I look down and see the murmur of my bones
like deep water, like wind. My sons play the long
slope toward the shallows of Lake Sinclair. Darius
still young enough to be surprised by everything:
a flock of geese flying low, sudden splash
of stone. The way wind can wave and warp
everything. We stare as a house made of water
and light shakes, shimmers, fades completely,
to reappear, become the brief home
of Canadas, of clouds, a small jet, and of course
two small children, one thin and long as the first string
of my guitar, one thick as a hammered thump
on a box. Mine and not mine, continually
altering the rhythms. Across the lake someone begins
to play piano, Clair de Lune, then mid-phrase, Joplin
and I can't tell if the little boy in the house is dancing
or simply chilled by a breeze that shifts and darkens
him, a floating shadow like a veil dropped into water
takes on water and slowly sinks. If there is a pattern
here, I can't find it. Always one beat behind
and reaching like a man who thought he could play
with the best of them but can't really, can't match
the tempo shift. Doesn't know which string to hit
for what he thought was the foundation shifts,
is polyrhythmic and the house once he entered it,
not the destination but another frameless doorway
leading out and down and in.

Spontaneous Firing

Neuropathy, the doctor says, without expression. The body
shouting out its false report. *But nothing
is really wrong. Like a fire alarm going off because
the batteries are low.* Of course, no warning is false,
just late or premature, misheard or heard wrongly. Wood
wants to burn and burns and, like a poem, a flame
can leap a long way from its origins. Its logic

is its own. Somewhere, someone feels a stabbing in his chest.
The breath stops in a crib while parents sleep. Two girls
make it halfway down the steps, their lungs full
of smoke. Everything burns. I just feel it. A month ago,
down Chellis road at four in the morning, a house caught fire.
It burns still, smolders in the mind's thick peat. If I had not
been sleeping, I might have seen from my bedroom window,

a glowing just beyond the ridge—or maybe heard the shots
the whole town swears were there amid the pop and blast
of glass and falling beams. And maybe they were. For some
say last spring they heard the husband pointed a gun into the air

and screamed at the rain—police were called, a warning
issued, and then there were the rumors: a troubled
marriage, Debt. So when the papers named it "accident,"
cause of death, "asphyxia," no-one believed. They heard

what they heard. *And that man was crazy* a good friend
says. *Anyone could have seen it.* Even the minister
shakes his head. There has to be a reason. I nod. I know
more than I'm saying—yes, they're always there—the signs.
Like that numbness in your left arm. Is it a pinched nerve
like you tell yourself. Or maybe heartburn. Maybe a burning
more distinct. Is it bad wiring in the walls or in the chest?
From where and when will the flame leap, the muzzle flash?
Our knowledge works only in reverse. Like a poem, like
Prophecy. The fire has a logic. And like the body, wants to burn.

My Son, Five, Dancing

Out of empty bags and wrapping paper,
out of the split smile of the overripe
and dripping, out of quickness of lizards
and the long-legged walk of the heron
through fog. Out of hawk-flight, out
of dawn and into the shock of the cold
pond on the groin, and the lightning-
struck tree still thrumming and warm.

Once, on the long drive home from work
I watched an old man dance on the edge
of a bridge above the highway like
some God-stunned snake charmer,
chin lifted eyes raised and lost beyond
all fearful calls beside and below

—the held-breath of the world caught
on a wobbly pirouette, a heel raised

over absence. There is so much you see
and don't when you spin like a torn leaf
—when you wish to step up into wind
and be lost above rooftops.

Surfaces reflect refract and seem
to give. Until the window
fractures. And bone. But my son,

turning, and flapping the silk-
sail of the body flung
from great heights, will not settle

will not come down until the wind
in his lungs blows singing out
of blood of breath of rhythm of now

and to hell with his old man anyhow.

The Well

Beyond the field behind my house, I found
an abandoned well covered in old planks,
a blanket of moss and pine mulch. I could not
see to water but inhaled the rot and wet
and thought it might go down forever, curve
into a belly like the long-plumed throat of a loon.
Stone after stone I dropped into the earth,
and listened. No splash, no thud, no clack and clatter.
There, amid the pines and calls of birds
there was only the swallowing of stones
and the low long breathing of a boy.

Gospel

We shall gather at the river, yes, but also
at terminals and depots. We will stand
hands raised, dodging the sleet-spray
of taxis. Asleep on benches and up
against the soot-gray walls
of Greyhound stations from Nashville
to Flint. In packs, jostling
for the window seat, rolling
our eyes and sighing.
And we will carry everything we are
in bags *no taller than 22 inches, no wider
than 14 no deeper than 9.* We will come
together hurtling at killing speed
surrounded by unbreathable air and bitter
cold sunlight so bright it burns the corneas.
We will read our books and sleep,
gathered and dispersed; then, regrouped
at baggage claims and rental counters,
long-term parking on the margins
of the highways that would appear
as shining silver rivers, if only
they were clear of each and every
fitful one of us, traveling alone.

The Contortionists

Parentheses are jarring to the reader. The temptation to use parentheses is a clue that a sentence is becoming contorted, APA Style manual

Everything (that matters) happens (in parenthesis) on the margins (in the alleyways and basements) where something waits (and broods) its many voices grope (like virgins in the dark) echoing themselves in moans for all that we have pushed away (or lock inside the way the acrobat will bend and fold each bone and muscle of each limb into a small glass box before her slim wrist rises and the long pale fingers flip the lid down after her to click it shut so one strong man can swing her by the handle to the gasping of a titillated crowd) (only to unfurl herself again as if the body were no more a thing of bone and cartilage than silk drawn out by hands in acts of conjuring) all peoples need their revolutionaries (all cities need the ones who won't stay on the sidewalks or sit quiet on the bus but) (need that first blues-man who thought to sit there on the stoop and bend a string then thought again to drag a bottle neck along a note to make it cry and sing and need that song the way the worshipers in pews or on their knees or counting beads besides their beds all need their heretics) the ones who make things (break things) new like dervishes who spin until the universe (begins to warp and bend contort into another thing and then another until each movement) is a dance and all dances (praise and all words) poetry (especially the ones we didn't say that caught within our chests and throats) like sobs like laughter waiting to (re)make the world (im) possible (again).

Communion

At the grocery store, post office, public restrooms, we
take up as little space as possible, we pull ourselves
into ourselves, look away, stare longingly,
close our eyes, slide down into our seats, slip through
and into pockets. Illicit shameful things, we
move together but apart, mumbling to ourselves
our absolutions and sidle away, unnervingly. When all along
Route 60 caught in traffic, caught in lines, we move
like long notes wavering distinct above the melody.
In and out of pitch and almost

out of time at five p.m. in JB's Gentleman's Club, bodies
supplicate and wait for even the lightest touch
and touch, *you understand the rules?* the dancer
asks. The man nods, hands twitching at his sides.
At Gina's Lounge, someone pulls the lever
on the slot down and down and down,
until his eyes begin to water. The chat rooms are all
full tonight. The frequency of witness that is
not witness. The hum that is the chorus of who
would speak for us. Who at last will say will sing

this psalm of silences. Caesurae. Desperate, the out
of work nail technician throws open the door
of her Camry in the middle of the intersection where
her timing belt has snapped like a piano string,
like a wire deep within her chest. She shouts into her
cell. A chain grinds 'round an axle. A weight
lifts. An engine starts. A man says *I am so
tired, so hungry* and the street says *yes.*
A woman says *I am so cold,* and the night says *yes
yes.* The chassis rocks beneath us, the wind shakes
all the wires high above the boulevard, a chin lifts
up as if in prayer, and the lips say, *yes.*

Psalm 23

Eighteen wheelers lean close as they pass,
or stalk the rearview, hovering above the shadow
of my son—long rocked to sleep in the hollow
of this dark palm, this gorge we travel through
on 68. The semis reel me back, grow massive: chrome,
steel and predatory, with the whine of gravity,
a very great weight pressing twenty tons

to our backs like rough hands like shame—
half-buried things—how we find the ways to hurt
ourselves, each other. I have been—the boot
that blows the door from the hinges, from the frames.
I've been the hands held up against the rain
of blows. I've been the caller and the called
and like a hungry owl, followed the cry
to its source in the throat and the chest
of the child waking to a world he cannot see
beyond the light that freezes, shatters, breaks
apart and whirls in crystals as they sweep
and dance like galaxies blown across the tops

of trailers. And now I've been this man
who says, *Sleep now, sleep. It's OK,*
when you wake we will be home, my voice
become sure as any god who could ball
the whirling stars up with the snow and the night
itself, reach back and throw it far beyond
the firmament and over the tops of mountains,

and the caught breath of wolves,
and the woman who works the night shift
at the BP high up on the mountain, trying
to decide if she should brave the drive
or wait it out till morning. I have been this voice

that says *I know* and knows we can't know
anything. But listens, trying to resist the urge
to let go, shifting into higher gears that will not
hold us back but send us lurching into fall and let
the taut jaw slacken with release and slip
and spin. I've been this man afraid and rolling

toward home, my son in the backseat absent
as the dead and just as present—in the way love's
tethers rope us to this earth, ourselves,
the night—my fingers gripped around its wheel.

God's Bicycle

God is pedaling a bicycle down
Highway 32, traveling west toward
Cincinnati against traffic (of course).
The bicycle is red—one of the sit-down,
layback types with three wheels and
a basket on the front filled with groceries:
local eggs, milk, cheese, some bacon
(He hasn't been Kosher in years). A Bengals
pennant blows from the back (Who
knew?!) He looks much like you'd expect
—a fat, elderly, white guy with a soot-stained
beard, and the slightly crazed and haggard look

of the father of many (many) children when
the children figure out he loves them
and that really, there is little he can do—
a time-out here. A spanking there.
Even if the burning pit is real, he will not
drop them. So they fight and bicker,
pull at his ears, laugh at shouts and idle
threats, beat the dog, masturbate on
the toilet, in the closet, in the basement,
on his favorite couch when he's at work

and leave the stains for him to clean.
Saying, *I know what you've been up to*
I'm everywhere does nothing (since
the Puritans) but make them exhibitionists
or hypocrites, at best, voyeurs. And what
did all that watching do to him at last
but make his eyes sore. So he leans back
in his pajama pants and flannels, pedaling
his bicycle. His chin raised skyward so
he can't see into the windows, can't
meet the hungry stares, and it is

a miracle how he avoids collisions
(mostly) and keeps the world in orbit.
There is enough to do (*Get out*
of the way you crazy old), switching
gears from high to low, muttering,
as he goes, *I love you all I love*
you I love you I love you all I
love you

MUCH

Warning Signs

When we speak of "safe" and "unsafe" as more than signs shaken by the wind—
     how they might be
a kind of ward, a warning, a benediction granted if we could hang them in a
     classroom or an alleyway or from
the one streetlamp blooming in the parking lot across 5th avenue, I think of the
     signs I saw as a boy in fields
behind my house: "Danger!" "Warning!" "Violators

Will Be Prosecuted!" And how I would step over or between them, fishing pole
     and net in hand, taking the shortcut
along the electrical towers to the glacial pond surrounded by scrub-oak and pine—
     one end
of a rope tied to a thick branch arced lazily above dark water in sunlight. The other
     wrapped around another sign: "No
Swimming!" Because a word can seem reality, a fist, when it is only a child's sketch
     of a hand. Because a sign
can only seem—is halfway, in-between, slippery, and

that's its power. Sometimes we'd sit, stripped, dripping on the banks and tell each
     other stories of a body found
floating, having somehow worked its way from whatever the killer had tied around
     its feet and swum up, shoeless
sexless, bloated beyond description, recognition, and we'd shiver, blue lips
     quivering. Sometimes the thought that we
are fragile—in body, in spirit—is thrilling. And strength

a kind of body language. The abdomen tightening, a flexed calf, a lip curled up in
     the ecstasy
of a scream, as the body flies up and out, mirrored over water for an instant,
stopped mid-air with the contrails and the clouds and the hawk,
     before gravity, before *make sure you're home before*
Dinner. Or what? *Or else.* But jogging, sprinting anyway

spooled out of and into a lengthening shadow. Before consequences. Knowing
     there are consequences, especially

when there aren't. Angler, swimmer, flier if I could only weave the words that
   would protect you, I would but

this sign around my neck that says "safe" might also read as

"warning" that you never were or are.

Redemption Center

I remember hunting soda cans along the edges of the strip mall parking lot, fingers sticky with sugar and oil, turning shades of black and orange as I tipped hot syrup into a hissing puddle on the blacktop. *Five cents a "pop"* the huge sweating man behind the counter liked to say, cheeks shaking at the pun. But it was no joke as I leaned into the counter, waiting for him to count them up—I always knew I'd need to get my hands a little dirty to get what I wanted. And what did I care if a schoolmate cruising past in the plush velvet of his father's Continental pointed and laughed at my garbage bags and dirty jeans, my t-shirt stained with grease and filth? Two hundred cans. Ten bucks. Just enough for a movie ticket and popcorn. Sometimes I still long for it—the simple return, when the deep dive of a theater on a sweaty summer afternoon and my head, swimming in the cool dark, seemed all the compensation I could ever need, and all I could afford.

52

Jack Coffey Landscaping and Tree Service, July 1989

He said we were going to do it anyway, do it now. He had a steaming heap of asphalt in the bed already and though the sun was hot in a clear blue summer sky so humid you felt greased and loose, he felt in his shoulders, the pressure of coming rain. It wouldn't, couldn't wait or we'd lose the day. Lose the heat, the job and that stinking slurry of oil and stone and sand would cool and harden to a crust and then what? *This is gonna suck,* Joey Fontez said. *Man*

oh Man, pulling on his gloves, tying his bandanna around his face. As Jack's sister Lisa smoked her cigarette, grunted, and shook her head—mumbling something beneath her breath. The chutes had failed to rise, no matter how much muscle or violence we used to force them, and you couldn't just lower the gate and drop the pavement where it was, pooling on the driveway and into the fine, manicured green of the lawn. *This rich asshole would have a heart attack, shit himself, and die right here in front of the whole damned neighborhood. Not good for business. Not good*

at all. We'd have to shovel it out. So Jack grabbed the asphalt lute, handed Lisa a smoothing blade and waved the two of us up on top, into the fumes and the stink. I remember the way things swam and ran: the greens and blues and whites of the suburbs, the red of Joey's Flannel, black of tar sloughing

and calving like a glacier, the scrape of iron on iron, and curses echoing around the oven of the bed, and then the way one gull overhead split into two then three and those cries expanded in my chest, flowering with heat, and how my body went boneless, slick, and sinewy and I was flashing like a pike in a bucket emptied into a river that fed into an ocean with the whole sky dancing on its surface—

a long thin muscle in flight.

Long after we had scraped that truck-bed clean and Jack and Lisa had smoothed the driveway flat, black as the Mystic at night, I sat on a rich man's steps with my boot soles melted away. *Sometimes,* Jack said, *you get so deep in the shit the only way out is to grab a shovel.* I took my first long drag from Lisa's cigarette. Neither fully in the shit nor out of it but high and flying, flowering, dizzy, breathing

the poison in.

Jupiter, Desire, Hope

5/26/2020

we duck and cover   our mouths we carry   ourselves with us
everywhere we are   we go   flames un   furled un   der the shadows
of flags shuddering from heat rising we have been called   to account called
home called   back from backyards and ballfields, boys and girls riding on
our handlebars. Sometimes I think   we never left our childhood until
just   now. Sometimes I think we'll never   emerge. And right now all
I can think of are   bikes left tipped on their sides on basketball courts.
Sometimes I wake in the night and swear I heard someone call my name, but
Rachael is asleep, and the house is still and quiet. *Auditory hallucinations* Rachael says
everybody   has them and I think   of the time I woke in bed as a child
and I swear I felt someone's hands around my neck and I couldn't scream and
whoever it was   was laughing and to this day I don't know what it was
I was hearing but I didn't imagine it and now it feels like   a pattern like things
coming together like   all these threads were waiting to be pulled or
plucked like   this dark melody was always floating right in front   of
me and around me and now we are all   entangled. I have read how slave-
ship captains worked the taverns of Bristol, Swansea, Liverpool, paying off the
barkeeps to run tabs all night long until   a sailor was both drunk and so far
underwater he could never reach   the surface (if he could swim at all) and
then, hit him   with the bill and threats   of jail, and a raised wooden
club. That's when the captain walked in the door with money to cover all debts
—and a job. The worst in the world, carrying men and women by force across an
ocean of disease and heat and fear, sharks following the wakes—of ships with
names like Jupiter,   Desire,   Hope. If 100 sailors left the port, 30
would come home. Hardened and full   of thirst. And so, it was back to the
bars. Some learned   to enjoy the work, make a life of it, with dreams of
becoming   captain, maybe even own   the boat. Sailors,   sometimes
I think we are being woken   from our stupor, a club slapped to the polished
wood. The debt   come due. And sure, there is always someone pulling on
the

strings, always someone   further up the chains that we hear rattling. But we
keep walking up the gangplank, telling ourselves we never had   or have
a choice. *Did you ever think   this would happen in our lifetimes* Rachael asks me
as we adjust   our masks and cross the lot   to the grocery store. *Yes*
I hear myself respond, and almost hear   the echo of laughter, feel   my
own hands tighten   around my throat.

Catch and Release

Sometimes I struggle to forget myself in remembering what I've held and lost. The
     way
in calling for your touch, I am a body in the process of giving up the body as the
     fisherman entering a river
becomes the river. It is a near thing,

this casting. Releasing the right amount of line, to load the rod with weight and lift,
     to leave
all surfaces behind so it can sing like a whip and take me with it, drawing back until
     I am a balancing act mid
-air, slack, then taut in the pull of what was, is, and comes: line and load where
     things unfurl, unfold, so the lure that licks the air flies, floats
down soft to rest trembling on the skin of another world like a hand to the back
of a lover. And there are so many worlds shimmering, layered one
upon another. It takes an awful kind of gentleness, letting go while holding to
the line that links them, links me to

the many men I've been, the hands I've held, arms that took me in for a night, a
     day, a year, ten, too many long and lonely silences, beds I've wrecked, and
     cars, a marriage, flights I've taken over every continent, flights I missed,
     and meetings too, chances, the job I didn't take at the charter school in
     Michigan, jobs I took that damned near killed me, paving driveways,
     cleaning toilets, tree work, brickwork, selling sneakers at the mall, each kiss,
     some sad, some desperate, some sweet with bourbon, too many bourbons
     ordered neat in too many bars, the many songs I've played and sung with
     too many lead guitarists, too many love poems and far,

far too many elegies. Two sons. Two wives. Two lives converging at a trembling
     point. Searching
for equilibrium the way a man might stare at sun's first crescent on a river at dawn
     when he can still feel the halo of the moon and is stretched
like a shadow across a hundred feet of moving water, and the cold slows down the
     heart until he hears it in the cisterns
and the ventricles thump close as the bracken fern and muck dissolve into a fine
     mist rising with the swept back wings of a northern harrier reflected on the
     surface. Under it,

a single muscle moving in a field of flow, a pattern self-contained and undulant
    that waves us forward by flexing
back and upward through shafts and globes until we are caught and pulled

thrashing from this world. I wonder if my son was listening as I whispered *breathe
    in, breathe out, relax I've got you*, then slipped a hand away from the hollow of
    his back as he

arced up, arms spread, eyes encircled in watery light and shot with terror, flickering
    from me to something
in the sky, a dragonfly, or a bird, or the sun in its slow blinding course. Or was he
    beyond
listening. Beyond the spell of words as he
balanced there on the edge of panic, of joy. And what did he see if he saw at all as
    I backed away
in awe or was it just the inward staring wide-eyed shock of birth?

Wow! Signal: Dredging Light

I too am not a bit tamed—I too am untranslatable, Walt Whitman

When it comes, it finds me shin-deep in our creek as I bend my knees, lock elbows
        and strain to dig down and in, and
lift the tall grass from the water, heavy, sucking free the silt and sod and sediment,
        so when the storms of April arrive, the waters will not flood
my lawn and threaten the foundation of my home. Summer,
when everything sings and stings with its need to be
uncontained, and penetrate the skin. And I am

at once the man with the bad hip and clicking shoulder and
the teenager working for the landscaping company, his flannel caught on a branch
        as it dives into the chipper. And I am
screaming and spinning out of the shirt, away from the blades. And I am
a boy watching in wonder, his mother lift and turn and stretch across a high school
        stage in white tights and slippers, my sisters on either side, their long, thin
backs growing wings,
becoming birds that glide over the water, casting shadows that chase each other
        down the beach as I shout after them. *Slow down. Wait*
for me. And the hound howling for hours through the steam of evening from behind
        the gate of the neighbor's yard, straining at his leash. And

the sod, and the silt, and the grass—my hair as wet and heavy as the nearly
        drowned. But come back, gasping. Everything insisting I am
not confined in these yellow waders or this body or this creek. And the shovel

is not a shovel but a dish, glittering with stars which are the future and the past at
        once, sending their messages of birth and burial. Ear to the rail, cheekbone
        to the track, I receive, picking up vibrations that dance across the distances

and through the skull to the tongue with a tang of pomegranates reddening the
        lips: somewhere on the burning

sand of an ever-expanding beach, unmodulated waves that might have come from
        a light-house beacon somewhere in the constellation of Sagittarius strain
at full draw aiming arrows across the heavens, flash and turn, turn

and flash. Somewhere in Ohio the astronomer shot through
with wonder stares at a signal he's been waiting for without hope and desperate
       with need, works out the coordinates, searching for the source of what he
       sees. A message

undecodable can say anything, everything. Old gods, sing

the language of the sumac reaching for the water pipes beneath the basement,
       curled around the metal, tightening its grip

or how the starlings wheel in a single wave, a wing.
Play the notes in any sequence. I am feathered with your arrows. I am wading in
       the waters. I am dredging my creek
come down from the mountains, staggering
with light and heat.

BONE MUSIC

Astrocartography

1.

When I was ten, I won a contest with a friend for holding my breath under water.
It was a dare and I hated him for that, hated them, boys naked and shiv-
ering in the sun, pointing from the floating dock. Laughing. How they
knew how much I feared the water and the dark. That pressure in the
lungs and how the cold stung my eyes wide in the murk. After he exhaled,
exploding

up and out, I stayed down there for another 10 seconds just to make them worry,
just to make a point. Then swam up lazy, slow, drifting as globes of light
spun and streamed from my mouth and nose. For the rest of the day, I
saw stars floating on the periphery

of my vision. Sometimes

I still do.

2.

Like most I have survived things no one should. But here we are, aren't we?
Miracle of miracles. With another surgical scar, another loss, another
lesson that doesn't apply to any other situation and brains starved for
oxygen. I am trying

to believe that pressure and loss can focus the mind, or like the saints in a fire,
bring visions. Did they hold their breath as the smoke rose up or did they
welcome the heat into their lungs hoping to see God? It is terrifying

to drown and terrifying to live and terrifying how quickly we adapt as we pull
ourselves onto the dock as if nothing had happened, leaving a world
behind only to realize much later that parts of us are changed or gone.
And so

I can't let go even as I stare down at my empty hands, swimming toward
the bottom. I do not know what I hope to find. A single shoe unlaced, the
skeletons of fish, a sippy cup, a teddy bear, a reason. Searching out what's
missing? Diving into that tear

in the cosmos? Trying to recreate an ancient map of stars to guide us home.

A Cheap Hotel in Aqaba, 2/6/2004

Over a tea-stained sink I gather memory, cool water in cupped hands and dip my
    face to put out the sun
in my cheeks and forehead and back of the neck and maybe some shame in the
    way that Susan would lick a thumb
and finger to pinch the wick and turn a flame to a wavering ribbon that snakes
toward evening all along the avenue, Al Hussein Bin Ali. In the cheap hotel in
    Aqaba the air is thick
with cardamom and lamb, dripping from a thousand spits in a thousand shops
    that rattle through the souk with shouts and laughter bright as shanti bells.
    The unit in the window tilts
dangerous, and hums a cool damp pulse.
Sand is in our hair, our socks, our underwear, the lining of our coats. The boys
    already drift off in their cots, dreaming of stone the color of pale roses as
    they float and spin as if still
on the surface of water heavy with salt, miles to the north. And I can almost hear
Susan with her mother across the hall in another 15-dollar room. And I want
and do not want to know what they are talking about. It is not yet dark but drifting
in that direction and the women in their hijabs hold each other's hands as they
    walk into water to their knees, fully clothed. Somewhere
a man is heading out for another night's work in an old truck. He crouches, checks
    the sweepers, bangs a long pole on the undercarriage to shake off clumps of
    dirt. Coughs, lights one of a thousand cigarettes smoked down to the filters
    or unfiltered, to the lips. Tonight
the highway of the Kings is clean and clear of sand
and accidents and ghosts of prophets traveling. Tonight
we sleep apart in separate rooms. Tonight
we long for something which seems far off as the memory of the scent of smoke
    or steam somewhere in a city that does nothing but call us to windows we
    can't see out of or beyond, any more
than we can see through dreams of children or lovers on their last night together
    and apart. (I wish
I could remember, how we came undone. But
I can only say that it was like
watching an accident happen from a mile away or sleeping through it in the
    backseat as the night goes tumbling. Slow and fast at once and terrible)—

a matter of one being near the end of things and the other, not yet beginning and
     with no way of catching up. (My son and I will spend
the rest of our lives chasing that ribbon down that busy street). Tonight
the cheap hotels of Aqaba all hum and lean toward
the city which leans toward
the sea, listening.

Any Moonwalker Can Tell You (it has a smell)

It has a smell, a scent—floating in on solar winds, star-sputtering from surfaces
       of stone, following you back
to the module, clinging to suits, to boots and bags. Born of meteors, and lava flows,
       sour with spent
cartridges and the barrels of guns. How a breath could tear apart the lungs, unzip
       the chromosomes,
how dust clung to everything, charged,

airborne. Back at mission control, in a haze of smoke, engineers and scientists
       smiled, nervous, laughed, lost
in a whirring clatter as equations kept on truing up—the craft did not sink into the
       powder, and the powder
carted back to a capsule full of oxygen did not smolder, burn, explode
like a star. Deep breaths all around. Easy to miss
a tickle in the back of the throat, a persistent

cough. What kills is never what we plan for. You have to look so close to see when
       change comes slow, and there's so much to blind us. After all,
on the bright side where there is no dusk, we are all
moonshot and shining on the sea of tranquility and the ocean of storms under a
       clear sky, black
as basalt, struck like matches, floating

like dust.

Alien Technology

Sometimes I want to take it all down to the studs, the way a kid on my block once took apart his deadbeat father's motorcycle (he'd been gone almost a month), using a ratchet set and tools found in the garage, sure he could put it back together exactly right if he placed each bolt, each nut, frame and fork, in a line on a blanket in the order in which it was unscrewed, and then worked backwards. *Reverse Engineering*, he told us. *This is what they do with the saucers they capture*, and we watched him grunt and sweat, covering his t-shirt and his jeans with grease, before we left him one by one, pedaling home before the early summer sun had passed below the tree-line.

Yesterday I heard an explosion, saw a sunburst flash into the darkness and then the lights on all the houses on our street went out at once. Later we would learn how a semi too big for the back-road along the highway had clipped an electrical wire and just kept going as everything stretched and popped, trailing and writhing behind in a shower of sparks. In memory

I move the scene back and forth, like a DJ in a dark club scratching a record in the middle of a song, the world astutter, askip. To find the moment there is no returning from and turn it like a dial or at least to see it as it comes, if it comes— to reproduce the solo as it was on the original recording, note for note. But we don't know by knowing. As if

in making love we could retrace our steps and bring the body to climax again and again as if it were all one body arcing to the tongue and worked the same way every time. Where would be the darkness and the sparks? We go and keep on going. And even if we could get that engine to restart, where are all the flying saucers? Tell me that? They should be everywhere.

All That is Holy

For the love of all that is holy, why? He'd shout, hammering a fist on the dash, staring
over the roofs of cars, craning his head out the window in a futile attempt to
see around the flatbed towing the doublewide into a one-lane merge on 93
just outside of Fitchburg at 5pm. *Jesus Christ, God*

Damn it to hell. My father who was and is forever in a hurry—even when he has
nowhere to go and the off-ramp is already far too close. The man who arrived
at his mother's wake an hour before the parlor had unlocked the doors so we
had to sit in the car listening to Elvis as the windshield fogged away the city of
Medford. *If you're not 15 minutes early,* he'd tell me, handing me a bucket of
balls on the way to the field before anyone else had even gotten to the locker-
room, *you're 30 minutes late.* And so I was and still I find myself

more often than not, shagging my own fly balls in an empty outfield, or counting
minutes, seconds, sometimes sweating or saying a prayer as I watch the clock.
Like a rigged explosion in a mineshaft, life as lit fuse. *Come on . . . Come on . . . .*
Do you start running or stomp it out? Or try to keep your eyes open as the
powder ignites and the air becomes a pressure wave alive with shrapnel? And
who isn't a little afraid

of such ravishment, tearing by us, through us past the speed of sound? All that
superheats the lungs. All that hits us all at once. The bullet strikes before we
hear the shot. For the little boy at the bottom of the pool desperate for oxygen
but holding his breath not wanting to lose the magic of the blue world he has
entered. And the couple holding hands in the waiting room of the cancer
treatment center. For

everyone anxious to get on with it and afraid of it coming, waiting for a chance to
speak while wishing for silence, starting up the car before we have our seat
belts on. Lord, how can I learn to slow it down, to touch and hold each
moment of this life, taking joy in making time, bending it to rhythm as hands
flutter like moth wings down the back to the base of the spine. So I am always

swinging a bucket of balls as I walk loose-limbed with my father just before the
start of summer and after the last bell has rung or watching Rachael brushing
off the beads of water after a bath, envying the towel.

Or sitting in traffic as I do now, the perfect light of evening shimmering every
burning hood and windshield

and all their colors flashing and shaking in the haze of summer into one sinuous
animal as it glides over smooth tar. For

the thwack and smack of wood on leather. For the blue sky that holds us for a
moment at the apex of its arc. For all that we have missed while waiting to
merge, not knowing how or why but only that this too, all this

must be holy.

Fire in the Cockpit
— Gus Grissom

We are all in space,
all the time she says, holding the hand of her wide-eyed son as they walk through
      the air
and space museum and I think of SETI and Solo and Kirk and Apollo
1 and 13 and the shuttle the earth would not set free and the one that broke
apart upon reentry. No wonder we long for some
swashbuckling captain to steer us through the asteroids on bravado and bluster,
      convinced of his own cleverness and unafraid. I think

of late winter nights, snow flurries whirling in the dark outside my frosted
      windows, and sneaking down to my father's den to watch, nose to screen,
      green skinned girls dance
and alien folk musicians sing and how, from my little capsule of a room in the split-
      level ranch on the gravel road behind the Kmart off of Main Street, I
      dreamed
of a universe that warm, familiar, full of life, which could be
traveled at warp speed, light speed, stars lengthening and streaming on either side
      so I might be

slung somehow unharmed across the great expanse of many galaxies. The Earth
      swings
around the Sun, a child spun in a circle at the end of his mother's hands, his feet
      raised off the ground and the Sun is whipped
around the center of the galaxy, and the Milky Way itself has let go, come free-falling,
      flying and it's all hurtling
through something, somewhere, like a car in stealth mode driven by some kid,
      hormone-high and whooping down an unlit street—lights off, windows
      down. It should be

enough the way we surf the hood, stars threading through our fingers. Must we
      always be pushing at the edges, trying to escape this world for another
      even as it takes us
pinballing away with the force of gravity and entropy and all the time
the heat is rising and there is nowhere to go, as everything begins to tremble and
      shake, lights flashing. Oh captain, what
was the last thing that you said before the flames filled the module, superheating
      the air? *We've got a fire in the cockpit. Get us*
out of here.

RE: Like a Box

This box is not a box, not a coffin, not a cell, not a window that wills and welcomes light into your home, casting a perfect square of sleep onto the floor. This knot is not a knot. It's come undone. Laces, trailing in the wind, catch in the chain-drive, flipping the rider up and over the handlebars (the first of many times I've flown apart). A product of forgetting all I thought I knew, all that I forgot. Unraveling, (unmasking, unmaking). Houdini in the water-tank struggling to release his ankles from the stocks, works his magic, unsnaps the locks. Once as a boy I watched in awe as a man crawled from the black smoke of a burning car, pulling his body through the window as if out of the deep water and onto the dock. Once as a boy I walked into an almost empty church and saw a woman's voice leave her throat in a flight of wings that became a flock of blackbirds wheeling, beating against the windows and the walls. And I have seen my sons turn a cardboard box into a submarine, an airplane, a spaceship. And I have seen one of them made to disappear into a box beneath the ground but somehow when I speak to him, he's everywhere at once and uncontained, a rhythm sprung. This box is not a coffin. But what we would escape into and from—bodies transforming into wings and water and smoke. And if a poem is not salvation, it might just be its metaphor: it does what a metaphor does: sheds its skin and slides away, getting at a thing by traveling out, making connections, growing larger as it goes until it can hardly contain itself, seeking itself in other lives, rhythms, bodies, gods: (How the solo can almost unmake the song). We say the great ones played "outside the box," and that night on the little square of a stage in France in 65 when hell and hope was breaking everywhere Coltrane channeled the divine, dove deep into himself, and took off in a run, was thrown, flung, gone, not gone: a new mathematics in fevered notes that shivered up against each other, the possible impossible: multiphonic sheets of sound, overtones, reaching up and up and up and up into an almost painful wail: the pilot having flown too far into the outer edges of the atmosphere grown dizzy, forgetting the passengers, the earth itself, and dragging us with him, ready or not. And my God the stars, the stars—some already gone a millennium but sending their light on anyway, knowing how long it can take a message to find us, having faith it must. Some dying. Some not yet born. And in being born again, this poem is not a coffin, not a cell, not a box full of dust any more than a flower is—or a fire or the light of a long-dead star, or any great love. This poem will not click shut.

Any Moonwalker Can Tell You (to see the earth)

To see the earth and the sun in the same sky at the same time is to reach up with a
      mason jar and ask the gods

to fill it with our own reflection. This is the eye behind the other eye, corneas
      expanding. This is the sky, a series

of lenses telescoping backward over the alps and craters and the plains and all the
      planets. To stand inside outside

on the highest hillside with all our faith and fragility—lights glowing on, and off,
      and on again, silent, fireflying.

Going Sideways

That's when it all went sideways, he says, leaning forward in the rain, drawing deep on
his cigarette and it's funny how many things you think in a moment like that,
like *who says that* and *what does it mean?* Like wheels losing traction on a slick
road and the truck sliding ass-first down an embankment? Or how heat
lightning splits across an August evening sky,

cloud-leaping? Or how my son, one night in a desert, flew through a windshield,
shattering into memory. Or more, the way everything is always careening, the
way someone told me once how the galaxy is sliding, sideways across the
universe at murderous speed and all I could think was—*sideways? In relation to
what, exactly?* But sideways we are going, and I've already lost the thread of
my friend's story—which seems very important to him. This life has a way
of slipping

past our defenses. Sidling up, making its excuses, saying, *is this seat taken?* and sitting
before you can answer. A man stumbles off the curb with a *Trump That Bitch*
t-shirt riding halfway up his gut. I'm looking while not looking, trying not to
hope he gets hit by the truck with the testicles hanging off the back. So much
is a waiting for something crazy to happen or a waiting for something to end.
A wishing we could slip the moment we inhabit for a new city a new state of
being, a brand-new pair of pants.

Memory is like that, the mind refusing to stay where we are or where we are
going. Most animals move in the direction they are facing. Except for crabs
(which move sideways) and the naked mole rat of East Africa which has
evolved

to move backwards rapidly. The man has started to spin in a circle while drifting
into the middle of the street. Somehow no one is hitting him. Somehow no
one even blows a horn in warning, recognition. I imagine he's a mole-rat in a
Trump That Bitch t-shirt (I refuse to imagine him naked)

and laugh. And my friend says, *I know, right? It's funny.* And I say *yeah,* sure is. Because
whatever it is he's talking about now, I'm sure it's hilarious when seen from
the right perspective. *Can a naked mole-rat spin,* I wonder? And would it have

this Neo-from-the-Matrix-like ability to avoid getting run over while careening diagonally across an intersection? And just like that, the mole-rat-man becomes a galaxy.

Or just another version of me. Another iteration. One that managed to avoid collisions. So much

is just the way we form connections. Trying to make sense of things. Astrocartography. Charting our minds among the stars while the world wheels and spins. As a chubby boy of twelve, padded and sweating through late summer football practices, I learned to keep my head on a swivel. It is important to pay attention. Not only to what's ahead but behind and to either side flashing in from the corner of the eye. I do not travel backwards

easily. I circle back in widening arcs

to the same songs, the same pictures floating from between the covers of the same books, the same unfinished arguments,

to the same desert highway under the same stars reflected on the same dead sea. And wherever I am, I am always drifting off to sleep and my oldest son is always sitting up front, his head silhouetted, a shadow unshattering. And the van is going seventy toward Aqaba as the driver's chin dips toward his chest. Beyond our seeing, miles ahead, a truck is parked across the road. And I can't do anything. We will keep going forward until it is too late to turn. We will plow straight ahead and in and maybe spin until we stop again. And I will spend the rest of my life asleep while waking, listening while not listening, trying to escape from where I am and where I've been and will keep going (because I don't know how to stop) wishing somewhere back there somehow it could have all gone

sideways.

Arrhythmia

In memory everything seems to happen to music—Tennessee Williams
"Association" is not a luxury, but one of the very conditions and prerogatives of freedom
                                                                —Judith Butler

1.

There is a shyness and a wish in the song of tires on the interstate after rain—a
consoling shhh that settles like a hand on a shoulder or fingers gliding through a
child's hair or the soft roll of cymbals fading at the end of the last torch ballad an
hour past last call when everything is settling toward silence still swelling and
swollen with a promise it will come again. *It will come again,* I say, whispering. It is
almost rhythm almost pattern, illusory and pregnant. A shifting space between that
hesitates with all the love and lust of a back-line drummer on Bourbon Street. I
have never been a man to rest in silences and sometimes I struggle to listen, to
wait. Too in love with my own voice shoving the silences away as if trying to answer
a question I was too afraid to ask my father my first girlfriend the homeless
man who flashed my first wife, Susan, at a bus-station in Omaha in 1998.
Or maybe I have always been asking just not waiting hurrying away to the
next appointment the next class, stepping onto the next bus, away from the
conversation, waving thoughts away through windows, half wondering at the
silent shapes those mouths have made.

2.

Yesterday while stepping into the office, a cry cut the air, making me stop and
turn—my hand still reaching for the door, foot caught mid-step. Behind me, only
the avenue churning with engines and students weaving through them, and one
old, heavy woman in a long white coat pushing a wheeled chrome walking cage
and leaning into it as if against a strong wind. I thought, a crow maybe, or a child
shouting through the backseat window, for no reason at all except for being that
child in that car or maybe just to startle a preoccupied professor late for class.
I almost turned again, then, *AIEEAAAAH.* Sharp and winged. The woman's head
tilted up, her gray hair hanging straight and heavy as a model's emerging from blue
water, her neck drawn lithe and taut. *AIEEAAAAH.* The note bending on a long
string, wavering. Then everything shifting back into that lumbering glide as if
nothing at all had happened as if *this happens all the time. It does.*

3.

For one year as a boy, I'd wake up screaming or wake myself with my screaming or my father terrified, hair matted and wild with sleep, would grip a damp shoulder shaking me until I stopped screaming. Not every night. Sometimes five days apart, then ten, fifteen, then back to five again. And once, three nights running. It got so he couldn't fall asleep or would wake for no reason at all, wondering if he heard me in his dreams, wandering up the stairs to my room, listening. He doesn't remember any of this. I don't remember the dreams.

4.

I fear most, not the forgetting but how it vanishes—erased, released so we might better keep our grip on what and who we would believe we were and are, the way the mind replaces what we see and hear and sense—adding details, writing over thoughts until it is another thing entirely. When does the name of the child separate from the child, become the only child—only the child—the photograph replace the skin alive with heat. So much is story. Words replace the blinding blue of a winter sky, the actual steam release of airbrakes, bloom of breath exhaust and bitterness of cigarettes which is a taste a touch a sound embodied and the body, a refracted image, broken into wholeness.

5.

Reaching back each thought of my father begins with music—Oldies 103 and winter trees blurring past us on 128 and cold vinyl seats, his warm baritone released in puffs as the Cavalier's engine worked to warm us, its wipers scraping frost as the heater growled and pulsed and clear glass bloomed up from the dash in a bright blue inverse cloud melting at the edges and we crooned with Elvis and Sinatra, my father's voice blending into the mix, matching tone and pitch as if it had all been engineered and I'd come in high and piercing, off, voice crackling like wet saplings in a fire and it was all fire and flashing windshields all around.

6.

I do not know if my son screamed when the van struck the truck, when the glass shattered around him when he was, for an instant, thrown to flight. I was asleep in back, until I wasn't. I did not hear and can't stop hearing. I did not see and can't stop seeing. Screaming. Singing.

7.

Ten steps and a cry again. Then five. Then fifteen and everyone looking away or down at their feet as she made her way past the student center and the purring SUVs and the CVS on 20th street. And for the rest of the day I found myself listening and waiting, wondering if I listened hard enough, could I hear it somewhere back behind everything behind the rumble of the air-conditioners and the chatter in the hallways and my lecture on Tennessee Williams and my voice speaking the words of Tennessee Williams which are too brutally beautiful to have ever been and I wrote them on the white-boards and the chalk-boards waiting and staring at the spaces between them listening in everything I heard and almost heard for the cry. In silence that isn't really— is only a hesitation under white-noise that's really just a blurring of a thousand pistons firing— a thousand small explosions blazing fast and indistinct. And is all of us and is always happening.

8.

And maybe it is all the same—same song, same cry, sung or would be if we could be listeners reaching down to the root of it—articulate—a shuddering with longing and maybe it is not our work to remember this and maybe the actual is ephemeral and maybe that's its beauty and ours is a different thing—the getting close while drifting back—the almost wavelike reaching of the sea, and maybe the best that we

can say is yesterday I heard this cry and I thought of my son, and it was like and it was like and it was like and it was like and it was like and it was like and it was like and it was

a bird bursting out of shards of light refracting stars over a desert into story into memory transformed, shapeless, shapely, taking on the body and ballast, the ballet of a boy thrown free of his body.

This is what listening means—finding in the storm, the harmony, the single tap of rain among the many rhythms, the molecule of hydrogen in silence beating like a heart among so many which is to find the unheard unuttered cry of one's own child in the eyes of a girl staring from a broken city, in a woman's unhinged wailing, in the body washed up on the beach a world away as the waves pound sand to sand drawn to and from the sea.

New and Bitter Flowers

We begin with the corpse of the deer in the road on the way to Lowes to buy new
and bitter flowers and herbs for the garden we had planted the evening before
only to wake with our morning coffee to stems of tulips and violas and the
ruined azalea chewed down to its bones—red and pink petals sprayed
everywhere. *It looks like a bomb went off in here,* Rachael said, as if she'd just
entered our son's room on a Saturday. *Damned deer!*

Which is to begin with two endings of two different stories that seem like the same
story because I can't see this deer without imagining him, alive and elegant
and with one or two others guided by the moon and the scent of blossom into
the sub-tropic warmth of our yard in summer, to chew on flowers as we slept.
And I wish I could have seen it. And wish I could get the image out of my
head. We can't

feel everything, can we? And sometimes aren't we blessed by what we don't have
to see? Imagine being so raw that each of our unnumbered dead shook us by
the shoulders, saying *wake up, wake up.* So raw that deer driven by hunger into
the human world dipping their heads only a few feet away from our beds to
feast would enter our sleep and tear it apart with their little teeth. So raw

that we had to think about each time we almost didn't make it to where we were
going, how close we have come to being clipped by the semi to be lifted and
spun toppling over and over like a doll dropped from the window of a car by
a child. Would we ever leave the safety of our rooms? Would we ever enter
them and risk closing the doors behind us? Could we even sleep? It is too
much

for any of us. And so, we plant marigolds and vincas, basil and rosemary
throughout the garden as if from them we might weave a dream-catcher to
fasten to the wall above a child's bed, as if dreams could be caught or warned
away or watched from safe distances. As if we were not all driven to the same
places by the same hungers. Or that we don't ache to wake one night among the
deer, awash in the moon, our mouths full of flowers.

Witness

-The ball I threw while playing in the park / Has not yet reached the ground

—Dylan Thomas

Once

from the edges of a pond out by the bogs I watched a dog break
through the ice. A big brown beast
of a mutt, chasing a yellow ball, had sprinted out too fast, too far, to where
the frosted white had gone to grey and black with shimmering. I remember how
     my own short breath
puffed clouds into a blinding chill that did not blind enough—a child trying to
     forget before the happening as if
you could unsee unhear unreal a thing, that you saw coming or if I turned and
     pedaled hard enough away or even closed my eyes, the ball would stop
mid-air, reverse its flight
or disappear and maybe I would not be there, having never taken the shortcut
     home from Pete's house through the woods
and never seen that dog, that ball. And somehow knowing even then how
     everything once touched must carry a scar. And we can't help
but be touched. He yelped and spun to splash in frozen sun—a ball locked in his
     jaws, and reached and reached again for edges
that splintered with his boy's laugh rising to a scream—brittle and blinding behind
     and out in front and everywhere

at once.

Suffering Tape

We have the tape. I don't want to hear the tape. No reason for me to hear the tape . . . because it's a suffering tape. It's a terrible tape. I've been fully briefed on it. There's no reason for me to hear it.—45

Sometimes I think I am haunted most by what I haven't heard. What is caught in the throat almost inaudible. Drowned out. Cut off. Mid

sentence. Pieced

apart and tossed away. Ignored. Sounds that are lost, like the voice of my oldest son on his 7th birthday. I know there is a tape of him singing somewhere but I haven't heard it. Don't want to.

As a boy I learned to sing by matching sounds—Sam, Aretha, Marvin, Otis, James Brown—reaching from the dashboard down into my chest until I hollered with them and the windows of the Chevy steamed. Dizzy, I could see myself spool out to blues and reds with golds of early evening sun and shadow as I shook and took the shape of starlings flocked or the flame of sunfish staring up at night from the windshield's blue-black pond, and dart off into fields of stars: that was long before I heard the chains rattling behind the chorus, long before

I learned what breaking meant, how it was transformation; it was crackling; it was resonant. How if you listen close/in/hard/far enough, if you stilled your breath, your beating blood, somewhere behind the chatter and the noise there would always be a keening always be a song. To be in rhythm is an act

of listening—to find the space between the blows, where we fit and where we don't and how to move and when

In a room somewhere

in the back of the consulate, the air conditioning purrs and swells then pulls back in upon itself as someone loops a cry, drops a beat (anything can be a drum, especially the body: the belly, the chest, the back of the skull). The quickened panting, *gasping* . . . and the fists keep

hammering. A crack of something precious, irreplaceable and soft. *I can't breathe, I can't breathe.* A scream. *Put your earphones in or listen to the music, like me.* Then the sound of listening

to ourselves. Where silence is made

of a hundred thousand choirs, a chorus of chainsaws. The hiss of a cassette. The groove running down. Static. Wind. An ocean.

We choose what we listen for and what we don't. Our record might just be

the damage we have done, debris

on the floor among the glass as the jets fly off—or

a cry thrown out of the body, into song.

What It Means to Drift

apart, to be a body as it slips away as if we were a mere suggestion of a gesture, a slow forming wave

goodbye or the promise of a swell that never crests. An old friend says the *man I knew died in the accident*. I think, at bottom

we are all bass, all rhythm or rhythms, high notes flashing on the surface of the sea, ranging rearranging, in any order any shape we can imagine as long as we remain

in time, in key. Someone suggests a phrase and that becomes a theme and then we play with it, build on that, going where it leads, and in the building make and take

away erasing as we add and add again until we've made

a brand "new" thing. The way that practiced fingers feel along the body's strings, down the belly, coalescing into shudder, moan, ululation, scream. It is a wonder

this becoming

and going and how it all takes on such weight. *The man I knew*

died in the accident. Thank God. New skin, new scars. Everything dying and being

born again—the big blue notes of misremembering. Mis

understanding our way to sense. Yesterday

my father kept repeating the same story as if in the telling he might make it stop

slipping away. I didn't say *you told me this already* or wish for who he was (who should be a memory?). But watched him search

the way skilled hands reach for a melody remembered from a dream. And find
   himself and lose himself. Somewhere, way down

the beach I heard a cry flung to the sea. It is a wonder how a sound can travel,
   becoming its momentum thickening, deepening, until it is its after-image.
   Sometimes

we have to see past all the echoes of what the gulls of evening scream. Sometimes
   I have to force myself to taste the salt-sting on the breeze. Until the sky above
   the bay is alive with singing, until I remember

that I've never seen this ocean and never will again. Always new, always changing.
   And my father

is saying *Son? Are you still there? Are you still listening?* And far beneath us
the world heaves, sand slip over sand.

Yes. I'm here. Right here. As you never were, we are. I am.

The Locomotive of the Lord

— *If the locomotive of the Lord runs us down, / we should give thanks that the end had magnitude*—Jack Gilbert

1.

I have never lived so far from the tracks I could not hear a train, its whistle and chug washing over me like dawn across an ocean or a prairie, if light could grow loud as it came on, or you could feel it rising in your feet, swelling in your chest, as if the train had started somewhere inside you as something small and far away and was growing closer, growing larger, so you want to dive out of the way, but you can't

dive away from yourself—it is always

too late. The mother pulls her child back from the tracks—even though he is already 10 feet away—her breath warm against his face, her lips close to his ear, saying *no honey, this is not the one, this is not our train* and his eyes widen in wonder at the sheer momentum, the speed and force of it, the flash of metal, its windows, blurring into a single sheath of all the tones of silver and the rushing sound and the bell ringing the end of the world and the feel of those fingers on his shoulders, tightening their grip, digging in, knowing how the train is not only the train but the space

it makes, the pressure wave, how it goes through you, and goes on, pulling you by the belt of your coat, lifting, longing to follow after it, so you must lean against/into its wind, then leaving you behind, unbalanced and dizzy in the settling of leaves and dust and longing, the gentle sadness and surprise that we are still here, that it has faded, that wherever it is going it is gone and you can't chase it, and whatever and whoever it carries away, it is not you and yet you feel

a part of you is going with it, the long string of your breath maybe, or a scrap of wonder that wonders if perhaps that was, in fact, your train.

Someone told me all metaphor is

2.

a proof for how the world connects or tries to. So, even the saddest darkest angriest poem is an act of love, an act of joy, lovemaking, being full of, being packed with, things, the stuff of life reaching for itself and for others, each thing getting as close at it can to the other things and throwing sparks. Dreaming of entering each other bodily then pulling away, sated and unsated. The sheets tangled around their feet. Maybe they tease each other about who will sleep in the wet spot. Maybe they spoon. Maybe they sleep. And on waking, reach for each other again.

I think

3.

of transfers and connections and tracks going everywhere, strong cables coupling cable-cars, coupling towns to cities, clasping the country together. As a boy I walked the tracks with my best friend and we'd put pennies on the rails, then wait. Placing our palms to steel to feel the first vibrations as if the train could ride our nerves, our veins, as if in feeling it miles away we were connected, boy to rail to train. As if we were the train. Then scrambling up the embankment, then the explosion, the roar of wheels and wind. I do not know what happened to those pennies, flat and curved, the fingernails of some bronze god, but I remember their smooth heat, alive in my hands.

And if I were to rise

4.

from this chair and wander like a desert saint, down the stairs and out of the house, barefoot, bareheaded, onto the damp road alive with stars, leaving behind this desk and this laptop and coffee mug, and the 1099s and W2s and the poetry book and guitar in the corner, impatiently leaning against the wall—like some teenager, bored and nervous—waiting for the press of strings to make them sing. If I were to get up mid-

line, and walk out through the woods down to the holler where the tracks are alive with the 765 rattling and steaming from Huntington toward Hurricane and step onto the ties, arms outstretched, legs apart in front of that train, to catch it and let it take me in one bright flash and the screaming of brakes

I can't help but wonder at the ways we seek that brightness, desperate for contact, grappling with the angels as they moan and scratch our backs and bite down on our shoulder-blades, at how we tear down roads too fast, and dive off of cliffs, and out of planes, taking the needle or the pipe or the pill, holding the smoke in our lungs as long as we can, falling into beds and out of them again, coupling to uncouple, and if we're lucky, walk away knowing you never really walk away which is, I think, a trying to unhitch, to interrupt the signal, the hive-like buzz, by going through a thing, feeling it completely and emerging, shaking off the salt and sea and drying in the wind and sun's heat, cleansed. To live for an instant, in the instant, with no expectations or regret. Someone else

read that book, pay those taxes. The guitar will be sold at the church yard sale to another skinny boy with long fingers and a head full of music who will play it better than you ever could with your heavy, brick-layer's hands. And it is a relief to know the world does not need us. That it might be better off, in fact. Have you ever seen a house off the road, overgrown with kudzu, so the edges are rounded and green and the shape

of a house is only a suggestion, discernable from a distance? Have you ever wanted to part the leaves and enter it, hot and dark like a lung? Loss can be a deepening too, the maker of poems and songs written by your wife or son and much better than yours with all their angry love and abandonment.

I know too much

5.
about this, I think. And nothing. I know it is a privilege

to be restless and dream of throwing a perfectly good life away. And I'm not going to. I am only saying

there is something about standing too close to the tracks as the ground begins to shake and the urge that it creates that reminds me

of good bourbon which reminds me of good sex and good poems which contain all the colors and flavors of sweat and risk (and the metaphors too) which makes you

want to dive into them. In front of them. Which is to say, there is something about the sound of a train.

After the accident

6.

when I was still relearning how to walk (there is so much I should explain) and couldn't drive and needed crutches to stand and swayed and ached with every tug and wobble of the world and was always in pain and Darius was little, only four. We rode the Amtrak from White River Junction down to Newark to visit Susan's parents, rumbling through the green-gray hills of Western Mass. into Springfield through the chill concrete of mid-December. I had to get up early from my seat each time we had to change a train and it was cold in the vestibule between the cars and everything creaked and shook and rattled and the walls and floors shifted and vibrated. And it was hard to balance, so Darius kept tightening his grip around my leg. And the ticket agent came to check on us, *Sir? Are you ok?* And I said yes because what else could I say (there is so much I could explain). And I remember never wanting to reach that station, get off that train, but to stand there in the iron cage and ache with my boy's death-grip on a shattered hip, wanting to tell him to hold on with all his fear and strength and never let go. And I remember how he looked up at me through his wild hair, shivering, and how his looking ran me down and ran me through. Sometimes I don't know if grief may be love's measure or maybe just a part of this, that unrelenting pressure on a healing break, a muscle trying to reknit itself as the cosmos shakes.

There is so much

7.

I can't explain—anymore than I can translate the language of a mountain, its trees ablaze with wings, how love like pain like hunger makes us strangers to ourselves, and makes us do strange things: steal and plead, and suffer, and dance like David to the trumpets in the street, sharpening our senses as we lose our sense, making visions come, so I wake in the night, certain I am still in the house in Georgia with the yard full of chiggers and the chain-link fence where kudzu grows and creeps and the railroad tracks behind it are always on the verge of humming and trembling into life so that all the China rattles in the cabinet and Susan shifts and groans, her long black hair spread on the sheets like a downed raven's wing spread across a highway. I have heard the voice of the son I lost so many times and have risen from the bed and tried to find his room only to stop and stare about in disbelief at who and where I was and then slide down the wall, shaking, grateful, sick in the gut, sweating, chilled. This life is a beautiful

accident made of accidents we try to shape. And sometimes the sound of your son in the night is the distant whistle of a train rolling away.

After the honeymoon Rachael and I rode the Wolverine from Chicago

8.

back to Kalamazoo. It snowed through the service at St. Mark's in Coldwater, through the reception, and the wedding night, and breakfast at her parents' farm, and the three days in the city spent mostly in hotel rooms. Glass boxes within boxes stacked on boxes, hovering over other boxes. All of them shining with their own light and heat and lights of the city. Warm spaces floating in the freezing air. Like stars among stars. If stars were packed close as they seem from a distance. Instead of millions of miles and years way. Separated by freezing space. How do I explain?

Do you ever think of her when you are making love to me?

and I said *no* (it's like an ache, this ache at my hip maybe; she is there but over there and still inside of me and all around but not). You can make love in grief, in pain. You can dance to the Lord in a crowd and still be dancing as if they were not there, as if He weren't watching, as if She were watching (we do it all the time) make love in a box of warm air in a building full of other boxes other people, clicking through the channels, showering, making their plans for dinner, dressing for the show, undressing for each other, teasingly, slow, or quick and desperate. I think of Susan. I think of Cyrus in the way you think of deer on a hillside outside a bedroom, throwing on the floodlights as you sleep. You know that they are there and sometimes you would wish to run a hand across a back, feel their bones and heat,
their hunger but you can't and sometimes you wake and stare and lock eyes for a minute and then they run off, run away.

And so

9.

we drank champagne we snuggled in a coat as the train plowed through two feet
of powder on a clear blue day and the snow exploded and whirled around us, caught in the wind that the train had made

around the train, glittering in brilliant constellations, a comet entering the atmosphere. A tunnel of sunlight, starlight, and frost wheeling and dancing in space

I have been thrown onto the tracks and run through, felt the blast of it, the heat and shudder, and have risen to find myself in disbelief, uncoupled

bones, reaching for each other for themselves, only to be run down again and that is how it is, for most of us, I think. Unless

you are lucky and find yourself one day shivering, someone whispering *this is the one. This is us, our train* and then maybe you step off the platform and step up onto the stairs and find your seat. And you think, I will ride this wherever it takes and be thankful. Thankful for the hand in your hand and the blazing world outside your window picking up speed as it goes, losing its shape, becoming a wash of white and green and blue and gray. Thankful

for the city and the buried fields of wheat and corn. Thankful

for the son you've lost in a shower of sparks and the son waiting for you at the farm and how sometimes you find one in the other. How one hand becomes another, sometimes painful in their transformations, and how they slip from your grasp. Thankful

for the grinding ache that reminds you of who you were and are. Thankful

for the fleeting moments when you forget it's there. Thankful

for how it returns each morning as you rise from bed. Thankful for the impact and the magnitude

even as you hurtle toward your destination, knowing that you must

get off this train. Knowing you will

be run down and through

again.

STILL RUNNING

This Year's Child

Our house is still on fire . . . Your inaction is fueling the flames by the hour, and we are telling you to act as if you loved your children above all else.—Greta Thunberg

Really doesn't "get" our frustration, our determination that she stay quiet, in bed,
in place, locked in the car and staring out the back window as we scream
at each other in the parking lot of the Kroger. She slips the seatbelt going
75 in a snowstorm, crawls from the crib in the middle of the night, chas-
ing the cat down the stairs and into the cellar, and will not hold hands
when crossing the street, running off, through traffic, each step a heart-
beat, a sequence of minor accidents. This child

is tired of our warnings, our excuses, explanations. Tired of our being tired. Tired
of all the animated movies she's been dropped in front of and all their
fictive happy endings. Tired of how we keep pretending the world isn't
burning and we aren't holding matches to the drapes. And of pretending

she believes us. This child used to try to tell us things. But the frog she played with
until the little boy she liked snatched it from the grass and tossed it to the
street, won't come back to life again. This child used to ask so many
questions. But she's learned we aren't listening

to the smoke alarm's incessant screaming. So

she reaches for the sweaty hands of strangers, wall-eyed and dreamy, drifting down
the aisle so we have to chase her—on Wednesday morning, when we're on
our way to the restroom and have to be back at the office in fifteen
minutes, and our car is parked illegally. She will not wear a coat,

even on the coldest days, and runs out the door half-naked, slipping on black ice,
laughing, mittenless, a wicker basket full of little teeth and bones all waiting
to splinter. She is the bare foot on a bumblebee. She is the sliver. She, the
sting. Always fascinated

and practiced in our cruelties. She's memorized the phrasing, repeating what we're
saying when she plays with friends, who then repeat it to their parents.

Who text us,

complaining. *Where DID she learn such language?* She bites. She hits. Spits in
inappropriate places. Sips your beer when you're not looking. And will not
look

away. She just won't stop

wiggling, giggling, swearing. Even in church, especially in church, as the priest
recites the litany. She will not wipe the snot from her face. And is not open

to negotiation. After all, what is left to say? What is left that we can take away? The
sky, the trees, the bumblebees? And what sane person would believe in

any of our promises. Don't get me wrong I know what it's like to look your child
directly in the eyes and say everything will be ok in spite of all the evidence,
in the face of every danger—the water shutoff notice on the door, the
predatory purr of engines circling. *Everything will be ok,* I said, wanting to
believe it (and sometimes it was and sometimes I find that I'm still saying
it). *Now go outside, play with your friends* only to watch from the window,
scanning the yard like the inside of a prison. But

this child locks herself in the basement with our pills and cell-phones, and will not
answer

the door no matter what we say. (There's no such thing as child-proof. Not for this
generation).

Virtual Sermon, Easter 2020

Today we watched a priest deliver his homily to an empty church and it was as if
he didn't know   where to look or what to do with his hands he just
waved them around then   clasped them at the rope beneath his belly then
behind his back   and he looked at the camera then down then away
exactly like a kid caught in a lie   confronted by his parents. He said   *it's
like we're on a train and it's been moving   very fast and so it takes a long time to slow
down the train   slow down*   but I wasn't sure what this train had to do
with   resurrection or with the story   he was telling about   Mary
Magdalene not recognizing Jesus but I kept thinking about   what it might
look like from a hillside sloping down toward the tracks   a fast moving
train coming through   a station and each person framed   within a
single pane   of glass, the hillside a   blur to the passengers and the
passengers a   blur from the hillside   sitting on their benches staring
at devices, not knowing if they would   or should   or could get off
the train or where   or when or what   it would mean if the train
did stop and there was   no station. *Inside   the train,* he said *you cannot
feel   the speed* but you can feel the rattle   and the shake of iron over
iron steel on steel just like you can feel   the body shiver and this is why
I never could read on a train and I wonder if   he really meant to talk about
what it's like inside   an aircraft when there is no turbulence. And I thought
of how a plane   can't fly below a certain speed and Bernoulli's equation and
how lift   is achieved and I wondered if I'll ever fly again, see   the
world from above with own my eyes—   the farms   laid out in squares
of brown   and green, blue rivers snaking through the empty cities. *Slow
down,* he said. Sometimes I wonder   what all of this must look like from
space but there is no outside   the train,   the plane,   the
cockpit   and maybe that's the point he was trying   to make. Because
we can't control the speed; we can't   return to where things start. Alone
and together and hurtling along   *Slow down,* he said.   And it was as if
the message was not to us exactly but like the breathy pleading in the back of a car
in some parking lot.   We are caught up in something   none of us
is ready for. And I want   it to mean something. To matter. I want   to
remember every   motion every   movement every   name and
touch. Sometimes I think   that nothing is more beautiful   or tragic
than a bare back turned   in walking away and the urge to say,   *slow
down,*   *wait* the song having ended but not   the hurried beating
of the heart.

Still Running

It is true that everything connects. Everything cause and effects. Which is good

and terrifying. They find a hole in a child's heart and the first thing that we do is
 think about the creek in front of the house, its water churning, the
 abandoned chemical plant
upstream. The one they never bothered to tear apart. Is it too easy to say *my heart
 is riddled with holes?* Like Beatty and Dunaway
writhing in a dance of bullets. But if you trace the bullet back to the source. Well,
 that's a hell of a journey. There's a story. To enter
my territory, take what's mine, all you need to do, is pay attention to
 the way my voice will rise or fall without reason, or how I get lost in words
or let them lose me, constantly leading us off the subject, off the scent. *My life's
an open book*, I say with open hands, *Really, you can buy it.* Few people do. And that's
 a blessing, too. There was a time

after I was pulled from the van, and back up into consciousness then rose from
 the bed to stand and then put down the cane, then walked then ran. When
 every step
was a gift. Just taking a deep breath in sunlight, revelation. And I remember crying
every day, as much for joy as anything. Which is hard
to say. Embarrassing, really. Shameful, even. How happy I was
to be alive, even with nerves like shattered glass in the gears and all
the nightmares. And my oldest son and my wife in the ground. I remember that
 first time

I tried to drive after the accident. I had to ride the brake with my left foot, accelerate
 with the right. And it was stop
and go for sure, and I was loaded up with oxy and an absolute menace to everyone
 else on the road. And yes, I'm aware of the irony. But no-one thought to
 take
away my license, and I was taking all back roads. And it was May, and the sun was
 out and southern Massachusetts was just starting to get the warm wet
heat of summer. That dewy perspiration, beading on its chest. And I swore
that with the windows open I could almost breathe the ocean. I had one hand on

the wheel and the other gripping a vanilla cream
doughnut and sugar was all over my hands and face and on either side of me, the
world blurred green and gold and the Rolling Stones' "She's a Rainbow"
blasted from the stereo. Why is every gift loaded with the fear of its loss? And so,
the convict never really escapes—

even after the bullets stop and the car rolls off the road into the ditch, engine still
running—the tide pulling at your heels, the beach suddenly distant. And
maybe that's the secret. That's the difference between joy
and bliss. My secret is
I've always been, will always be
afraid—each day emerging, as an act of desperation. My secret is, I could not love
you without first and always imagining you

gone.

The Wave

Once more the heat on the back of my neck, early June, and I am moving to and through my own unwhistled tune across the parking lot to my car, a bop in my step despite my hip, a bottle of wine in one paper bag, a block of cheese in the other and for a moment I'm letting myself feel good in spite of everything—and everything is a lot these days: a new war in Europe, the virus, Arbery, the opioid crisis, my father's cancer, his dementia, Roe v. Wade, in no particular order—so much you half expect the Ohio to run red and skies to fill with locusts. Every new story competing like a sign, a signal, a siren among sirens. It almost makes you want to remove the batteries from your smoke alarms. And in this small Appalachian city there is always a siren, always something to alarm. So much that it feels bad to feel good—even for a second. But today, right now, I am generous, loose with summer and even the scent of exhaust is sweet and if I could, I would

uncork the bottle right here in the street and pass it to anyone who asks, I'd put Curtis on my car stereo, turn up the bass, and let it play until my battery died and night came on and I had to wobble home drunk. I'd grab the hand of the old woman in the bright sunflower shift and dance her away from her walker, let her lean against my body as we rock, my nose pressed to the top of her head. But there's never a corkscrew around when you need it

is there? So I smile at a child, she smiles back, and we both ignore her father's stare, his *whatyoulookinat*. Until I realize I'm still wearing a mask and tear it off, like a boy pulling off his shirt to dive into a public pool. And maybe this is why the strung-out woman in the hello-kitty hoodie walks up when she does, arms wrapped 'round herself. And I can tell she's been using, maybe pills, maybe horse. She's got that jittery shaky thing going and she's too thin and her hair is lank with sweat. And I know she doesn't need money for gas, or for a bus ticket or for the little girl she says is waiting in a minivan she vaguely points toward. But I honestly wish I had some cash—because there's something inti-mate about being on the wrong end of a hustle when you and the grifter know and everyone around you knows exactly what this is about. If not, every booth at the state fair would be empty, and no one would bother to vote, think about it. I even consider handing her my good bottle of wine, cutting out the middleman. I can buy another and why shouldn't she get to feel good for a minute, but I know it would be only a minute, and would be the most irresponsible thing I could do so I wave her away, telling her the truth, I have no cash to give and she looks at me as if to say, We both know you're lying which is ironic in so many ways. But I put the groceries in the back and fire up the engine, the seats hot and sticky and I think

of my son, 21 at school in Boston and wish I were in Boston and 21 again, barhopping down Boylston Street in the early evening with my friends, breathing the salt of the ocean in along with the stink of garbage cans and hoagies sold from food carts on the sidewalk. And I think of the last time

I was there with my father. It was August 2021, in that brief stay of execution when the numbers were going down and people were getting vaccinated, and we were all feeling a little hopeful and maybe reckless and so I got us tickets to a Red Sox game. I gave him his shot of Lovenox in the Prudential parking garage (he was having his blood clots then) and we limped our way down to Fenway, the two of us talking about how good it felt to walk in the middle of a crowd again, to move with the wave and not have to think about where we were going, just letting it carry us with it toward the banks of lights and the Citgo sign. And people happy and smiling at each other—groups of girls in summer shorts dancing in the middle of the street, recording it all on their phones. And how he spent the whole night complaining about

the seats I got behind the net on the first base side, and the starting pitcher who let up three home runs in the first two innings, and the guy two rows in front who wouldn't *just sit the hell down fah chrise-sake,* and we drank watery beer in paper cups, and he kept calling me Herbie for some reason. *Herbino,* he said slapping me on the shoulder,

and I let it go because whenever, wherever that was, I could tell that they were in a good place. And we cheered and we laughed. We even got up for the wave each time it came around. Because I think we both knew that all waves dissipate. And this was only a moment but a hell of a good one. And the Sox came back and won, and it was great.

Moonshot and Shining-New Poems

Snowblind

Every waking is to strangeness—a realignment, an awkward reconciliation of the
    branches of the body, these bones and nerves that seem
so ready to splinter under the burden and brittleness of frost. I think of how my
    father struggles with the static
in his head as if he's always on the edge
of going under, or coming back
from strong medication. Or like a man digging through a snowbank trying to clear
    a path
only he can't see where he's going, and the snow keeps blowing back
into his face. How sometimes he will linger in that space
between. And there are nights when he has thrown himself across the bed, diving

toward the plate in some game a part of him is always playing, only to batter his
    head
on the baseboard (he was only trying to slide in
safe). Last night I woke in the storm to silence. The world become
a bowl, emptied into another bowl. And I kept trying to flick on the light.
Staring at my hand in disbelief. As if my hand
were the problem

and not the storm, the ice, the glazed branches, the snow
that weighted them, to break the power lines and throw a county
into cold. I just kept hitting the switch. As if that would make
a difference. As if I could

unbruise my mother's arms. The memory of the times my father
jumped out of bed and ran outside into the parking lot shouting

call 911 Now. Someone's stolen the car even though the car was right there. And my
mother saying: *it's scary, Jo, what happens to his eyes   open   but not seeing
or seeing   things that are not there   or are there only   in his head.   It's
like he's searching   for something. Some thread. But it's broken or   he's lost it. He's
lost. And it scares me   to wake him and when   I get him back to bed, I'm scared
to fall   asleep.*

When I was a boy, a blizzard
tore through the country dropping five feet of snow and drifts
of seven up against the sides of houses so my father had to exit

from the second floor and dig a tunnel down
the stairs from the back porch and around our home

to the door. And when he finally pushed and puffed it in
with a crunch and a pop, coming through the light, blinding
with snow, he handed me a shovel—a plastic thing made for a little boy.
Jesus, he said. Steam coming off him. Glittering. Laughing. *What a storm.*

Confessional

I remember the stone, staring up at me from the ground, smooth and silver in the light and flecked with bits of quartz. I don't remember picking it up, only that I'd had enough of being the target. Of being the one who got laughed at. Pushed from behind "accidentally" on the stairs, in the lunch line, waiting for the bus. I never talked back. Never stood up. So I picked up that stone, closed my eyes, and threw. She was fifty yards away, and over forty years ago. I remember watching it arc across the patch of blue sky between the red brick of the school and yellow leaves of fall—or was it spring and green? It was a mean thing to do. She was a mean girl. And I loved her in the way kids love. From a distance. Without hope. She said something cruel. I don't remember what it was, but it felt at the time like the closing of a door. Final like that. She must have noticed how I'd stared at her, as if trying to memorize each black curl. Each motion and move of her delicate knees and elbows, the gleam of shoulders in the sun. And I was quiet and strange and often lost in my thoughts. And all that looking must have made her uncomfortable. And maybe she just wanted the looking to stop. And though I wasn't the only one who looked, I was the least desirable, or maybe just the easiest to confront. And damn it, I'd had enough. To this day, I feel the wonder and beauty of it, that stone impossibly arcing its way toward love and thinking there is no way, no way I could hit her from this distance in this breeze without even really trying, and with my eyes actually closed, and, Please God, wishing as it flew that it would miss the mark. It didn't. It was a miracle. And I remember the moment of contact with that perfect shoulder. The strange intimacy of it. The interrupted laughter I thought was aimed at me and how it became a scream. I don't remember her name or the punishment. Only that I was punished. Only that everyone seemed surprised—the girl and the teachers and my parents and everyone else on the playground—and how for a minute it felt good to feel dangerous. To have people wonder what I might be capable of. I've never stopped wondering.

The Evening Before Your Biopsy

we spend pulling weeds from lemon coral we've coaxed along the edge
of our lawn. You make me wear a bucket hat to keep me from a sun
that has already disappeared below the tree line, and a long-sleeved orange shirt
        and gloves so I look like a human
traffic cone. You tell me to keep my ass out of the road, and to stay the hell away
from the poison ivy and Virginia creeper because my skin reacts to
everything. I tell you
to stay off the stone wall above the creek where you

are pulling vines *you'll break your neck* and then the image of that happening fills my
        mind: you toppling
down headfirst, then unmoving and broken in the creek, and I won't let it
go until you are back on the ground. *Ok. Ok. I'll stop. You win.*

But what would you have done if I weren't here? It is a wet heat, and my sweat-stung eyes
        weep with lotion, so I have to keep reminding myself to keep
my hands away from my face. But I know I'll come in
streaked and filthy from the cheekbones down. I can't help myself

from plunging my fingers into the ground, abandoning the hoe and trowel,
digging for the root of the crabgrass. I'm so tired
of protecting myself
from everything. 52 and double-boosted, obsessively masked and still I got sick,
        and it's been three weeks and still I'm exhausted and

no matter how old I get a part of me is shirtless and 19, digging a flower bed into
        a rich man's perfectly manicured lawn, leaning on a shovel, thin
and glistening, burning the acne from my shoulders, until the skin peels and
        bubbles.

In the center of the yard, a dead Japanese Maple has stopped winding leafless,
        upward around its imaginary post. I have promised you
I'd cut it down, but I never find the time, only an excuse: *what do we do about the
        stump?*

Once it starts to go, a landscaper told us, snapping a brittle branch like bone, *it goes.
Everything lives and dies. Even trees.*

And it did. One branch failing to leaf, then another. But I can't stop thinking
that I must be responsible somehow. The way I grieved each joint I smoked that
      year we tried to get pregnant. It scares me

how my hip and knees and shoulders ache these days or how long it takes for things
      to heal. I can feel
the day come on when they won't
and how the decade between us will ache
like an ocean. How a tree can go from blooming red, its canopy spreading six feet
      in every direction,
to barren and grey as stone and how it happened
so quickly and in slow motion right
in front of us while we watched from the window.

Unmarked Graves

Like unsigned poems are everywhere in everything, the center
of a sentence unsighed, the chains of a hoop still rattling long after
the ball has passed through on its perfect arc. We half-see
in the place we pass through—a haunting that is only a space
where something else has lived, still resonant. Whitman said
to look for him beneath our feet in the dust rising. To believe
that we are made of Whitman dust, in dusk, stars flickering. We
carry the ache of our own loss like someone searching for the keys
he is holding in his fist or the glasses still perched upon his head.
Loose in a boy's limbs, sheened in sweat, his birth. On a path a mile
or so off Main Street, behind the church, under the apple tree
you find each name your father has forgotten will forget: the first
few moments at the end of a story when it starts to change and
shift the leaves above your head, alight, alive, marked by the wind.

The Edges of Things

I miss the time when the world was only blurry at the edges

of things. In the corner of the eye where I once thought ghosts lived. And when
ghosts were only something

that hovered on the periphery. Not in but outside parentheses. Something to be
thrilled by, laughing. Hiding beneath

a fortress of blankets with my sisters when my parents had turned the lights off in
their room in the renovated basement. A signal

that we were on our own and should not bother them unless it was an emergency.
And by emergency, I mean

house-fire. Home invasion. Nuclear Armageddon. Not a monster beneath the bed.
Not a bad dream.

Now every night I feel ghosts rising like the bones in Ezekiel's valley—they are
dancing. Now I want to throw

the lights on, screaming, *Lord let my bones be boiled and bleached and played, a chiming,*
percussive fill in the break that knocks you in the hips, drops you to your

knees. When did I begin to have to hold the page further and further away to make
out the meaning? It makes me think of how my father's reading glasses
began to gather in the strangest places. All over the house. On top of the

toilet. In the crisping drawer of the refrigerator. On the label of a record still
spinning. Maybe it is always about this urge to

see which is an urge to hold on to someone

something as it slowly drifts down these rivers beyond our hands beyond our

noticing. Which is to say, I noticed, but didn't quite

believe, telling myself I could still reach out and pull you back whenever I wanted.
Now

I see ghosts everywhere, in everything. And it has been a long time since I believed

In anything I see, never mind my reach. And I'm telling you it scares me. And Jesus
but I miss my sisters.

Cosmic Hum

The whole universe is humming. Actually, the whole universe is Mongolian throat singing. Every star, every planet, every continent, every building, every person is vibrating along to the slow cosmic beat.—Adam Frank

In the early 1920s the Soviets outlawed this kind of singing, naming it ritual, magic,
    superstition. And it is

strange to hear so many voices emerge from one throat at once in a guttural choir. Music
    has always been a threat to those who do not know

they are dancing. It is hard to give in to the beat but harder to know you have done so
    already. Moving to a melody just beneath the surface of things,

we've adjusted to the frequency, all of us vibrating all the time together, riding the
    gravitational waves in space-time that set the universe

to shaking. As for me, it's been years since I've gone dancing, my hips cannot unlock
    themselves and I'm troubled by sore feet. I was never that good to begin with—
    too conscious of being

seen in the crowded gymnasium, too prone to think my date might be laughing at me. And
    then there was all that

sweating. But my mother and my sisters were dancers, still are, and I love to watch them,
    love to feel the rhythm come through me. If you stand in the middle

of Beale Street on a Saturday night when the music is coming at you from both sides,
    guitars layering on guitars, fifty sets of drums, and all that bass it's like the city has
    a pulse,

a heartbeat. And I've always loved to sing. It is not so much that I'm uncomfortable with
    silence it's just that I've never believed in it. Except maybe in space. What would
    it mean

to channel the echoes of stars dying and being born? To voice a billion tones at once,
    one throat an orchestra? Maybe it would sound like this, like listening.

After the occupation, as the last tanks rolled away, they say the air was full of humming

Any Moonwalker Can Tell You (of the silence in static)

of the silences in static, its wintry flakes and the time it takes a breath to freeze
and float

away. When you are almost afraid to make the shapes of sound, the mouth a
blinding sun in blackness that is all night

all day (or is it the other way around?). How everyone is waiting and everything a
countdown

as a boy who struck the hammer on his thumb waits for the pain to dissipate but
it takes so long from 100

to 1 and father saying *you can get through anything if you take it a second at a time*, lowering
the little hand into the bowl

of ice. When hope is circling miles up and a million millions things must go right
to even make it to the next beat

of the heart. So many times I've watched myself go down, slipping on a sheet of
ice under snow, felt the crunch

and shift of bone. And how I'd listen to Elvis singing on the little yellow Walkman
I'd bought at K Mart with the money from my paper route, his voice

like a whistle down a tunnel or a loon-cry over water—that distant, soaking wet,
and close as I pedaled my ten-speed through December and all the way

to June when the moon hung low in the sky just looming there too close and much
too far

to touch like every girl I'd already fallen in love with dreamed about

and father telling me how *the whole world stopped but not like it did for Bobby or Martin
or John it was all of us watching at once and we were*

scared for them and for ourselves but also proud and kind of brave like we were, for the first time, emerging from something, some long sleep and I mean it was

the moon and I remember the lift-off and the touchdown and then, they were walking around on the surface and how it looked like a beach and how we

cheered over beer in the basement. We had this cheap set, black and white with a monster antenna and a big dial on it that never seemed to do very much but I

couldn't keep my hands off it and your mother and I were living in California, and it was

a bright sunny day but we kept looking at the TV then looking out the window to the sky. There's no way

to tell you about it. I mean, it was the moon far and close, big as tomorrow.

Any Moonwalker Can Tell You (while circling the dark side)

while circling   the dark side, out of contact with command, Apollo 10
started picking up   a signal—whirring, whistling   *strange sounds in a
strange place*. A strange land. Strangers, desperate just to see the earth reappear
on a horizon, silent, bristling with messages, how   many signs have been
shaped to our need for touch   fingertip to fingertip with a reaching hand?
O, to be   grabbed around the wrist, pulled up and out.   Even if there
is no way   to process it, there is always   oscillation, vibration, everywhere
a shaking. Deep inside the body, inside the module there is a pulse/impulse. There
is   anticipation—everything on   the verge and   waiting for
someone or something   to shape it. You can travel in silence, planet
to moon and back, or like forgotten cosmonauts   ride   the   comet
screaming all the way into the vacuum. We believe to be heard is to be
seen is to   connect—charged particles interacting as a wave,   then
scattering again. And we know how dangerous   that can be—this urge to see
        an absence and reach   into it—to begin to hear in nothing
everything,   mistake each echo in the emptiness for a sign   calling us
out into oceans, caves, alleyways   we've convinced ourselves are tugging
at our coat-sleeve. And the music? Scientists   would claim it was
only interference: two radio   signals inhabiting the same sonic space.
Symphonies   have been created   out of less.

Any Moonwalker Can Tell You (about the poetics of space)

All these constellations are yours, they exist in you; outside your love they have no reality!
                                        — Milosz

About the poetics of space. Bachelard would say,

that every person staring out the window is displaced in place, the universe outside the
        glass rippling away from an imagined center, a

dream state—each leaf on the hillside rustling with reverie, in the way

a candle flame can set an angel spinning and flashing on a carousel of tin. Each
        little room

a universe: the piled papers on the desk, the cooling coffee cup among the empty
        coffee cups, the browning overwatered spider plants which, if understood for
        all their history

would tell not just one story, but everything back to the first footprint in the dust, the
        first flower blooming outward ever-expanding

        to the last sun's death. But it also works the other way— immensity on all
sides pointing,

        pushing in. The zero-gravity

of consciousness that comes at sundown to one who struggles to remember a
        place, a name. His shadow somehow separating from his feet to flee as if
        chased, as if a river were to gather itself behind it and run off on its own
        current so he

could never step into its waters again. And who are we without that turning back,
        that stepping in that lets you know yourself again, your story. I wonder

trapped in their protective suits staring through their plastic shells toward home, 251,000 miles away,

did the men on that cold rock feel the joy of solitude, those waters spread

for miles in every direction among stars floating and flying— and stretch

their arms and leap

like divers from some cliff. Or reflecting on the tiny ball so far away

half-swallowed in their own open mouths, were they

afraid?

Any Moonwalker Can Tell You (about the black expanse of space)

What I saw was blackness and death and the deep coldness of space
                                        —William Shatner

about the black expanse of space

which is not the absence of light but of atmosphere, an emptiness, a

lack of any way for light to reflect refract and scatter in shades of blue or melt into
        hues of red above the Oceanus Procellarum as our shared sun sinks behind
        the peaks of the great Apennine Mountain range. And though the stars
        seem everywhere, they are so far

away they can't illuminate any more than Christmas lights strung outside your
        grandma's trailer, or summer fireflies in a field. So far, we judge their
        distance by the time it takes their light to reach us. So we are always

looking into the past but seeing in the present. And those stars are traveling away
        as if someone had tried to throw us a ball from a flatbed going 75 on
        the interstate. Or maybe the way

the siren of an ambulance will stretch quiet, lowering in pitch and dissipate even
        though it is still screaming its warning. The message it carries/carried
        already bouncing down the highway and off to rest among wildflowers, the
        messenger,

a memory. The doppler effect. This morning

my father locked himself in the concrete storage space leading up from the
        basement to the backyard where we'd spent the morning stacking wood as
        I'd done so many times as a child. And if it weren't for the way he wobbled

when he walked or chose only the lightest logs or had to use his weight to swing
        them up and into place, or had to pause to get his breath and so hardly
        spoke at all no matter how prompted (the descent

into silence a product fear—of saying the same thing he had already said, then
    realizing it, in shame. (*I'm sorry, my brain*

doesn't always work the way it should these days) it could have been any of those crackling
    winter days, father and son, taking turns to push

the wheelbarrow to the back of the house stacking firewood in the alcove by the
    stairs. When the last log was set in place, I leaned the barrow against the
    house and left him at the bottom of the steps, turning with a wave, *I think*
    that should do.

Sure, that should get us through the winter. Sometimes I hardly know

what it is I'm looking at or listening to. How to tell the afterimage from the thing
    itself, the sound from the note still playing only in my head, sometimes I
    don't know who is pushing the wheelbarrow, and who is walking behind
    or ahead. (*I'm sorry. My brain*

doesn't always work the way it should.) When Rachael asked me, *what's that? Do you hear*
    that? There it is

again. I had an image of my father on his knees by the stove with his little hatchet
    making kindling from the drier logs. *Just dad, building a fire* I said. *Thump,*
    thump. Thump,

thump. Mistaking what I remembered for what thought I knew. Until finally I heard
    the almost buried *let me out let me out* and ran downstairs and yanked the
    door in with a rush

of cold to find him shivering, scared, and angry, snot and tears streaking his face.
    You locked me in. Where were you. Couldn't you hear? You couldn't hear me? I was
    screaming. Christ, I was pounding on the door.

Sorry, I said, again and again. And didn't explain how I never closed or locked
    anything or how I did and didn't hear him or maybe didn't want to.

And didn't try to show him all he had to do was climb the stairs, turn the handle
  and pull, then step right out into that bright cold afternoon. Or
  how much it scared me right then to imagine him

turning in place, with no star to guide him, screaming for help. Locked

in the space of darkness in the darkness

of space.

Any Moonwalker Can Tell You (or, Earth to Joel)

how it feels   when silence means you might be a   drift. On your
own   out there. And I think how much fear can be conveyed in the
cutting   of a cord. How fragile we can be in the absence   of a
corresponding voice or even   a dial-tone,   silence,   an open mouth,
a   swallowing   that lets you know that something's coming and what's coming
can't be good.   *Hello?*   *Hello?* I have learned there are questions I don't
want the answers to. *Joel, I know you are confused. That's the drugs. You're at Kings Hos-
pital. There was an accident, Joel. Darius is going to be ok. But Susie and Cyrus. They didn't
make it, Joel.* And so   I am   always speaking across the void and having to
fill the silence on my own to find the right words and have them at the ready   as
if a word   could speak the capsule through the atmosphere bring   a
body back through the windshield   piece the glass together like a memory
that leaves your hands   stinging with blood. My mother calls in the middle
of the night, *We had an accident, Jo,* saying   *you have to talk   to your
father*   who is in the hospital in Brockton after falling down the stairs   again
but thinks he is somewhere   else and wants to go   home, swears there's
nothing wrong   with him *or* his brain. *I'm only 45* he says, *too young   to be
living like this.* And suddenly, in this moment, I am

older than my father and   somehow   still his son only I am   14 and
he's saying   *Joel,*   *are you still with me* as I stare straight though or past
him or out   the window slack-jawed, *spacing   out, a space   cadet,* the
way   I sometimes did   and do when too many things converge
connect overwhelm

shoosh-of-tires-heater's-hum-siren-song-lyric-guitar-solo-drums-red-sox-game-
gull-cry-jet-hornblare-ticking-of-a-turning-signal-mosquito-buzz-breath-last-two-
lines-of-a-poem:

his impatient *Joel?* an error code on an alarm   *Joel   Joel?*

A crack in that glass, the silence that is sound   static   white noise my
name a question which was and is always   somewhere in   my head. And
ready to go   off. *You there, kid? Earth   to Joel.* I don't know how   to

respond. I am everywhere and   nowhere. Each moment calling to another as if they are embedded in each other: the first son in the second, marriage within marriage, father in son. Times I have called them by wrong names: Susie/Rachael, Cyrus/Darius. Each word each step a motion forward dragging loss along and out in front. Maybe time has no meaning on the surface   of the moon. Or maybe it is all you have,   all that matters. Time   measured in oxygen   in fuel in   heartbeats   in the distance between call

and response. Or maybe it's all one moment in the way that Dylan said it's all one   song   that to compose is just a matter of   pulling it gently down from wherever it's floating up there   unthreading it from a skyful of notes of   seconds strung like constellated stars on the sur- face of an ocean   like plucking the flightpath of a

bird from a flock. The journey of a leaf torn free from a storm. Which may be to say there is no   silence   not where there is   life. Once,

by a lake on a mountain in the heat of summer I lost   Darius. Which is to say he was there and then there was a crowd and then he was not   anywhere I could find him. That no one there with me, even Rachael   seemed to know where he was or had an answer to *Where is my son?!* no matter how frantic the repetition   was,   increasing   in   volume   and   pitch

WHERE   *is my son?! Where is my*   *SON?!* And here I could try to tell you what it's like to "lose" a child and to be   lost to   him to   wake up in a hospital to find him   gone and wonder

if he is somewhere out there a   drift calling my name because   I know that silence   too. Silence as a waiting   for response. Darius

was found that day, though still I wake sometimes in the dark, shouting *Where is my son?* And Rachael frightened, and silent, hand reaching out but   waiting not knowing how   to ask *Which*   *one?*

Any Moonwalker Can Tell You (there is no sound on the moon)

There is no sound on the moon. Too little atmosphere and yet they say it rung
like a bell when they crashed the lunar module into it (on purpose)—the way
some angry kid might wreck a car he's hotwired, knowing he can't keep it,
knowing there would be a reckoning. So, having torn up the grass of every field
in town, and driven wild down every private road, the radio turned all the way
up, windows wide open, he takes it to the top of a hill, throws it into neutral,
then hops out,

running. I have had my bell rung too many times to count, only to be sent
back into the game, across the brittle grass of the high school football field,
having guessed right at the number of fingers, the day, where I was and what
I was doing. (what *was* I doing?) First, I should say, how much we didn't know—
that this was normal. And you can't really blame the coach (who was, more
often than not, a father) for doing what coaches, what fathers do, teaching

a boy to get back up off the ground, looking into eyes that were once his own,
telling himself there is no damage done because there was no damage done
to him. *So get back out there, son.* Not knowing or admitting if ever how long
far off the reckoning would come. And it always comes. It's enough to make you
scream

your lungs out only no one can hear you above the roaring the ringing,
concussions and repercussions all around. Shuddering in place.
When the module struck, it hit with the force of a ton of TNT, the reactions,
seismic, and the moon vibrated for over an hour—so long, some wondered
if it might be hollow. When you strike a thing that hard there is always
a consequence, even if you can't hear it, even if there is no bruise, something

that can be measured not just by the damage done but its reverberations singing
back through space a quavering note which goes on and on long after everything

beneath the surface settles to new places though it looks the same with the same
smooth, blank look on so many smooth, blank faces, long after the impact has
come

and gone, long after the father forgets the name of the son, and we've left so many
footprints like scars upon the surface of the moon.

How to Walk in Space: Untethering

A good man's life is never quite ended—Ed White, American Astronaut

1.

At your bedside, as you came awake, I found myself
looking down and away. You mumbled something. My sister said, *yeah, we know*
     dad, you're ok. You're OK. As if she knew the language of the dying well
     enough to translate. As you fell
asleep, we spoke of how the nurses would increase the morphine and lorazepam
     drip by drip until you'd just drift off and away like a windborne puff
     of dandelion seed.
And I thought of those first spacewalkers stepping out from the hatch, a gold-
     plated umbilicus, providing breath, while keeping the body tied to the
     ship. Lifeline
and leash at once and all of it circling, tangling, flashing with no up or down to go
     by but the blue earth and white of the sun, visors
ablaze.

2.

When you first came here, you wouldn't stop trying to rise, to pull the IV from
     your arm. I thought of your father in his last days, how he'd beg you
     to *just please*
take him *out of this place*
to get ice cream as I sat in my chair, lost in the cloud
of my parka, sweating and staring at you both, wanting
you to say *Sure, Dad. Yeah. Let's go.*

3.

And still, I imagine us stealing a wheelchair, charging down the hall and out the big
     glass doors, into the cold bright winter,
laughing and lifting, carrying him to the car to speed away, down Route 1 to
     Friendly's for a sundae, nurses shouting and waving
in our wake.

4.

All boats tug at their moorings, kites at their strings, even flags fray, threads
     unraveling in the wind: when he had to return

to the capsule, Ed White said it was the saddest moment of his life. And the
    volunteer

who sometimes sat with you when no-one else was there, told us of the many who
    seemed to wait until the family was gone to take that last breath and let

go. And that's how it happened. I want
to believe

5.
you were OK. More enraptured, than afraid. Though I have lived enough to know
    these expressions
often share the same face—eyes wide, mouth agape. The boy clings to a rope
as it swings above the mirror of evening, sun and boy

and moon at once reflected in the deep blue surface of the lake. I want

6.
to believe
it wasn't just about gravity, the silhouette of a body pulled through the
    vacuum of space, spinning uncontrollably, but a leap

from the rope's full height and length, fingers unclasping, a gathering of
    muscles folding at the waist into a dive into

the sky, headfirst, a cry of terror

and delight, an act

of grace, which is release, releasing me as the rope goes slack, swings back to my
    hands,
empty, reaching from the beach. There are so many ties that hold us

here, in place, when all our choices seem to lead to the same destination. Life
works that way

sometimes. So does love.

O Rings

Trying to come grips with the psychology of machines,

Norman Mailer (being Mailer) brought it back to sex—everything and everyone an
     interface—a connection—a kiss—a link—but

any moonwalker can tell you how carefully each move must be made, a balletic
     transposition, a pirouette in space, how everything must be aligned,
     perfectly—the pilot careful not to oversteer or use too much thrust—
     trusting entropy to do its work, to dock—the way

my mother used to bring the boat in, killing the engine, spinning the wheel with an
     offhand, last-second flourish to glide in stern-first toward the moorings,
     with only a gentle wake lapping at the dock: the complex mathematics of
     intuition overcoming distance and resistance to bring together in

compatible parts—a thing we used to call seduction (Were we ever that
innocent?)—so like

a writer to imagine a world of wants—all the stones intent on the caress of a river,
     the crowbar a crack beneath a windowpane, the trigger, pressure, the fist,
     a chin—a moon, its planet—"Now" become another word for waiting on
     the surface as your lifeboat orbits overhead—each stage of the ship,
     desiring, reaching, aching like an astronaut for home, for each other—but
     also, themselves—to be a thing and part of a thing at once is to be

conflicted—is to be constantly making

messages and waiting

for translation before they are received, then waiting again—and to wait is to be

locked in an embrace with an unknowable thing—which is maybe why Collins
     claimed he never felt lonely through the 27 hours and 14 trips around that
     rock (*I had too much to do*)—self-contained with containment, within

his capsule, the radio cutting out, kept company only by the beating of his heart,
     his own body's stink, a light the console blinking—isolation as freedom—
     after all he wasn't the one staring up at the sky in faith and trust—like
     children staring out into a parking lot, an hour past the time when their
     parents were supposed to pick them up—or a parent when their child is
     the last one off the bus—in the space before

a rendezvous—when there is only you

and your wanting and how each wanting contains

consequence—any interface must find, must create, space, gaps, points

of contact—must translate, conduct information, energy across

the gap—everything a semicolon, or better, a dash—the Russians could never
     crack it—their N1 splitting at the seams, exploding on the launchpad—
     I think

of all those early fumbling attempts in the passenger seat of my father's Chevy in
     the parking lot outside the abandoned Brothers of the Sacred

Heart Catholic School for Boys—and of that light that blinks

and blinks its way each morning outside my office window, along the
     mountainside, across the Ohio—

lonely satellite—and I can't help

but wonder what driver plows through the dark, what kind of person steers what
     kind of machine toward where, by when— and why that connection matters—
     what is the payload—what is the spark

traveling a wire or leaping branch to branch, sky to surface, launchpad

to space—a cup of coffee set between thick thighs, nestled to the groin and
     steaming—the engine trembling the surface—and I think of those O Rings
     and the sequence it took, it takes, to blow it all up—a few degrees of cold,

the seal compresses, and gas escapes, ignites—then

poof—then

boom—so like a human, balancing

its wants, clinging for dear life to itself and to others, waiting for it all to come

apart.

How to Walk in Space: 3:35AM Dec 9, 2022

My feeling was, I was a grain of sand—Alexie Leonov, first man to walk in space.

I wasn't asleep when the light came on and you filled the doorway, *it's happened Jo,* you said, *oh my God, oh my God* and I don't remember getting out of bed or walking toward you or anything I said if I said anything what is there to say but I came to you in that hallway *what do I do now. What do I do?* And I put my arms around you while yours hung heavy at your side and you leaned toward me while pulling away as if afraid the embrace

would make it real. And you shook and language failed. Your sob, the groan a ship might make in a middle of a storm as it takes on water and weight and started to sink, and I could not tell if we were stepping out or in or just away or were suddenly weightless holding on to remain in orbit. Where flight and floating and freefall, stillness and speed are the same and the enemy is entropy. When you start to spin, and you can't

come out of it. The first cosmonaut to walk in space was out there for only twelve minutes and he almost died, the oxygen meant to keep him alive expanding in his suit because of the difference in pressure, his hands pushed from his gloves, his feet from his boots until he had to open a latch from his suit and bleed the air into space just so he could fit back through the airlock and slam the hatch behind him. And then there's you, having spent how many years circling around him and the last few trying to navigate with everything gone wrong, unable to control

your flight, or trust in gravity. You would be the first to say so much of it was beautiful: moments even at the end, when he'd try to smile and pull you in to dance and start to sing, and though he'd mostly rock and swing in place, hardly able to stand or move his hips, it was like the sun coming up over the edge of the world your whole life turning beneath you. I wonder what is more frightening: to watch someone float away or be the one

adrift. And so, I drove you down the frozen road to his body and we spoke of how you almost felt relieved and hated yourself for that. How in those last few weeks you'd come to dread each sundowning and how the night would come and threaten to pull you both into its darkness. And how he kept asking to be driven

home when he was sitting right there in his living room. *It's time for me to go*, he said. *I can't stay here.* And nothing anyone could say could make him believe. Even when we walked him down his own front steps and turned him around to stare at the house he'd spent half a century in. With you. *This isn't my home* he said. And maybe it wasn't anymore. Mother, I guess I want

to tell you that I don't know what heaven is or isn't or where but I believe in re-entry—the cleansing burn of atmosphere. I know a little of the fear of taking that first breath. You are not the first to have walked in space and found yourself ready to come back—seared and shining—

to this world again.

A Memory of the Sun

The body creaks, then cracks apart, thrumming like a drum beneath the ice—where
        every bone is a bell waiting to be struck, and every tendon tuned to the
        highest frequency, then plucked. Much of what I've lost is flexibility.
        Getting out of bed takes a plan, a plot. The nerve zinging up the leg,
        along the hamstring, to the spine. But also

much of the will to stretch, to reach for the branch that might hold the memory of
        the sun bent beneath the weight of leaves coated with ice. Once I was

a body walking along the frozen rivers beneath the bridges with a handful of stones.
        Every child born to winter knows not to step anywhere the water might
        be moving, no matter how far down it runs, but you can skip a stone along
        the surface like your father tapping on a wall, searching for a stud. And listen,

death is always an assumption and a good one, but

where there is life, there is always

an alarm going off, something hissing in the bones, in the blood that says not yet,
        not now, get up, get up. Listen, the gulls are crying all down the shore.
        Listen

once, I saw the body of a stray dog, still for hours and coated with frost shift then
        start, then shake, taking off in a run, ice crackling from its coat in a galaxy
        of sparks.

Acknowledgments

There are too many people to whom I am indebted and without whom this book would not exist. First, I should acknowledge the feedback and support I received each step along the way from Rachael Peckham and Darius Atefat-Peckham—incredible writers and readers as well as the great loves of my life. Special thanks also to Robert Vivian, Wendy Barker, Laura Michele Diener, Jeff Tigchelaar, Daniel Lassell, Sara Henning, Nicole Lawrence, Ryan Faulkner, Kayla Queen Dyer, Bethany Woods, Tony Viola, Eric Smith, Michele Schiavone, Mary Moore, Marie Manilla, S. Diane Wellman, Hank Stanton, H. Palmer Hall, Craig Challender, Art Stringer, Marc Harshman, Kevin Carollo, Nayt Lundquist, Travis Dolence, Lily Jurskis, Tawanda Mulalu, Christopher Kempf, and John Van Kirk, who all read and gave feedback on early versions of these poems. With love to my family, Jeanne Peckham, Tina Kemp, and Lisa Maidment. Love as well to all those I have played music with, especially Reuben Ambat, Eric Jonsson, Davis McGraw, John Salvage, Julia Grimmet, Stephanie Fernandes, John Fernandes, Andy Ambat, D.T., Reid Moak, Miles Sheft, Boscoe Sheff, Jared Allen, David Slitsky, and Drew Maidment. Eternal gratitude to Kimberly Verhines, and the entire staff at SFAUP for the work they have done on this manuscript. This collection is dedicated to the memory of my father, Joel Peckham Sr., and to my first mentor, Robert Pack. Finally, I write in memory of Susan Atefat-Peckham and Cyrus Atefat-Peckham.

Grateful acknowledgment is also given to the magazines and anthologies where many of the new poems were originally printed, sometimes in slightly different forms:

"Any Moonwalker Can Tell You (while circling the dark side)," *580 Split;* "The Evening Before Your Biopsy," *Another Chicago Magazine;* "Snowblind," *Contemporary Verse 2;* "Unmarked Graves," *The Christian Century;* "On the Edges of Things," *The Greensboro Review;* "A Memory of the Sun," *Jet Fuel Review;* "Any Moonwalker Can Tell You (there is no sound on the moon)" and "Any Moonwalker Can Tell You: O Rings," *The Nashville Review;* "Any Moonwalker Can Tell You (about the poetics of space)," *The New York Quarterly;* "Us And the Rain," *SLAB;* "Any Moonwalker Can Tell You (about the black expanse of space),"

Poetry Online; "Confessional," *The Southern Review*; "Any Moonwalker Can Tell You (of the silence in static)," *The Sugar House Review*; "How to Walk in Space: 3:35AM Dec 9ᐧ 2022," and "How to Walk in Space—Untethering," *Vita Poetica;* "Any Moonwalker Can Tell You: Earth to Joel," *The West Trade Review*.

Poems in the rest of the collection appeared originally in *580 Split, The Ampersand Review, The Anthology of New England Poetry (UP of New England), The Autoethnographer, The Baltimore Review, The Beloit Poetry Journal, The Black Warrior Review, Blueline, Borderlands: The Texas Poetry Review, Cave Wall, Cloudbank, The Cold Mountain Review, The Comstock Review, Confrontations Magazine, The Connecticut Review, The Connecticut River Review, The Edge, Every River On Earth (Ohio UP), The Florida Review, Full Circle Journal, Grist, Jelly Bucket, The Literary Review, The Louisville Review, The Macguffin, Mud Season Review, Many Mountains Moving, Nimrod, The New York Quarterly, The Orison Anthology, Onthebus, On Unity: Coming Together, Falling Apart (Mountain State Press), Passages North, Poets Against the War (Nation), Palooka, Prairie Schooner, Rattapallax, Rattle, The Raw Art Review, The Southeast Review, The Southern Review, Spillway, Storm Cellar, Tar River Poetry, Tiferet, The Valparaiso Poetry Review*, and *Without a Doubt: Poems Illustrating Faith (NYQ Books)*.